*Words, Words, Words*

# Words, Words, Words

## Essays and Memoirs

GEORGE BOWERING

*Vancouver*
*New Star Books*
2012

NEW STAR BOOKS LTD.
107 – 3477 Commercial Street | Vancouver, BC V5N 4E8   CANADA
1574 Gulf Road, #1517 | Point Roberts, WA 98281   USA
www.NewStarBooks.com | info@NewStarBooks.com

The publisher acknowledges the financial support of the Canada Council
for the Arts, the Government of Canada through the Canada Book Fund,
the British Columbia Arts Council, and the Government of British
Columbia through the Book Publishing Tax Credit.

Cataloguing information for this book is available from Library and
Archives Canada, www.collectionscanada.gc.ca.

Cover photo and design by Mark Mushet Photography
Printed and bound in Canada by Imprimerie Gauvin, Gatineau, QC
First printing, October 2012

# Contents

# Acknowledgments

Many of these pieces have appeared, usually in somewhat different form, in previous publications. My thanks to their editors:

*The Walrus*
*The Capilano Review*
*Rampike*
*Cottage Life*
BookThug
*The Al Purdy A Frame Anthology*, Harbour Publishing
*The Globe & Mail*
*The Ivory Thought*, University of Ottawa
*Olson*
*Dooney's Café*
*Open Letter*
*Matrix*
*The Heart Does Break*, Random House
*The Collected Books of Artie Gold*, Talonbooks
The Vancouver Canadians Souvenir Program

I'd like to say thanks to Karl Siegler,
who has been a great help for years.

*A Writer in the Family*

*When I was a young heroic writer on his way to the* pantheon, I told my mother over a midnight kitchen table that I would probably break her heart in some way if it meant that I could write something terrific, or even get the chance to write something terrific. Later, even after a thorough exposure to the English Romantic poets, I declared that I would rather go to heaven as a person than as a writer. Now in my mellow years I just write when I write and dote on my sweetheart Jean when I am doting.

## 1. *The family son*

I have often told the story of my stealing my dad's job as sportswriter for the Oliver *Chronicle* and the Penticton *Herald*. It was a double job: first you kept official score at the town baseball game or the high school basketball game; then you converted your coded research into breezy journalese, picking up tips from all the articles you had read in *Baseball Digest*.

Not only did I steal these jobs from my father, but I also used his wonderful typewriter to do them. I can't remember what brand it was, but it was probably about the third or fourth most popular brand — that's how we bought stuff in our family. It was a portable, and I used it the way my father did — taking off the cover but leaving the machine in the other half of the case. It had round keys with brass-coloured edges, and while it was black, some of the black had turned brown, the way that lovely old typewriters would do that.

I even typed the way my dad did. Once, in Grade 10 at school, I got punished for having all my homework done so that I could fool around in study hall, the punishment being that I had to attend the introductory typing class, something usually reserved for kids in 10C. I was the only kid there from 10A. Our school couldn't afford many typewriters, so a lot of our class time was spent poking fingers at a drawing of a keyboard on a piece of paper.

But I never learned to touch type. I saw my father hunting and pecking, his portable on a card table, as he wrote his baseball story, or typed up the minutes for his next Elks meeting, or created a chemistry exam for his Grade 11s. And here is the kicker: he typed with his two middle fingers, because he had cut off a lot of his right forefinger with a saw hooked up to a truck wheel. So back then I typed with my middle fingers, too. Everything I learned from him I did with my middle finger. For example, he was a shooting instructor, so I fired a .22 rifle with my middle finger. I tickled my girlfriend's palm with my middle finger. Eventually I smartened up — at this moment I am typing these words with my index fingers.

When I moved away from home at age seventeen, the first thing I saved for and bought myself was a portable typewriter.

But with my dad's typewriter, on a card table or out on the lawn, where I would get my picture taken, long-haired fellow sweating out the paragraphs, I could imagine making books, figuring out how to assemble gatherings of pages or signatures, not then knowing those words. The materiality of books also preoccupied me the other way 'round — when I was buying paperbacks at the drugstore or pool hall I was interested in the whole package, reading all the stuff in the front pages and the back pages, noticing whether there was stitching, as on White Circle paperbacks, seeing the way the cheapo brands had typefaces that looked like typewriter letters. When the New American Library Signet Books became higher in proportion to their breadth, I favoured Pocket Books and Bantam Books, that stayed short, but eventually they went for the higher shape as well.

I was a lone boy in all this. I had two friends, John Jalovec and Art Fraser, who gobbled up westerns and other paperbacks that were a long way from our English teachers' approval lists, but I never knew whether they were turning into writer boys. They certainly didn't write for the paper, or even the school paper. Despite all his typing my father never did any "creative" writing. No one else I knew in town did, except my buddy Willy's mother, who wrote some kids' stories for the weekend editions of the Vancouver *Province*.

So there was no "writing community" in Oliver, that's for sure. In fact it never entered my mind that such a thing was possible. There were no painters in town, as far as I knew, and certainly no place to see paintings. I once had a commission to do giant cartoons of the firemen for a firemen's ball, but I didn't even see those when they were installed. Outside of high school the only musicians I knew were a couple dance bands, one with accordions for polkas, the other with saxophones for other kinds of dancing, led by Gar McKinley, my high school music teacher. I was in the school band and the school choir, working off the bass clef for both of them.

I also wrote songs with my buddy Willy. Usually I would write the words and he would make up the melody. These were based on the model of the hit parade at the time — romantic love songs, two verses, a chorus, and a third verse. Later at university we wrote the songs for a musical comedy about the opening of Japan by the Americans in the nineteenth century. It featured great tunes, such as "I'm yo Daimyo" and "I'm the Shogun with the Slogan."

In high school Willy and I would hardly ever perform our songs, mainly because though Willy had a great voice, I was shy, partly because I knew I had more style than voice. But Willy and my girlfriend Wendy and another couple formed a quartet that I baptized The Troubadours, and *they* sometimes sang our songs.

But *I* knew all the words of all the songs on the hit parade. I still know most of those fifties songs, and so does my daughter, because I sang them with her when she was a kid. I don't know the words to any of today's songs — maybe they don't have words, I don't know. People were amazed that I'd memorized all those songs, but they never told me I should be a professional singer. In fact, years later, at reunions, they told me they thought I would have become a stand-up comedian.

I was an actor. In high school I was always in a play, on one occasion in two at once, dashing from rehearsal to rehearsal. I played the lead in Oscar Wilde's *The Importance of Being Earnest*, of all things. There was an adult acting organization in town, and though I went to their plays, I don't think I was ever in one of them, or was I?

Well, I wanted to do all those things — write, sing, paint, photograph (Willy and I had a darkroom in his basement), be in a band, whatever there was. But when you are in a small town, and you are the kind of kid who goes on mountain hikes alone, the one that is easiest to do is to write. You can keep it a secret. Unlike acting and singing and cracking wise and all those things, writing was something you could do alone. Besides, I had an inferiority complex and a superiority complex at the same time. I felt socially inferior and intellectually superior, and did everything I could to pretend the opposite.

But though I wrote some poems and stories when I was a high school kid, I imagined myself as a sportswriter. I collected sports magazines (I still have them packed away in boxes), so I knew the names of all the sportswriters in the United States. I even wrote to one I liked a lot, Bob Broeg of the St. Louis *Post-Dispatch*, asking him what I should do. He said to come to Columbus and the University of Missouri, the best journalism school in the USA. Of course I could not have afforded such a thing, even though my mother's family was from Missouri. Besides which, the girl I loved was going to go to normal school in Victoria. The normal school shared a building with Victoria College, and my uncle Jack lived within walking distance, so that's where I went. Clearly, I have made all the important decisions in my life for love.

## 2. *Country Boy in the World*

I had a less than brilliant year at college. Then I got a job up in far northern British Columbia, with a government surveying outfit, but I turned out to be an incompetent in the bush as far as the government was concerned, so I flew and hitchhiked back to Oliver with my caulked boots around my neck. Then my girlfriend said that she would have to be interested in a more mature fellow.

So I went to Vancouver with my buddy Fred, who had flunked out of flying school, and joined the Royal Canadian

Air Force. I was a photographer in the RCAF for three years, during which time I wrote amateurish adventure stories and got real rejection slips from *True* and *Saga*. I also wrote a weekly column for the *Rocketeer*, the base newspaper at RCAF Macdonald, Manitoba.

I came out of the air force twenty-one years old and in love with the idea of being a writer. I started keeping the poems I wrote instead of chucking them out. I had my air force clothes and a little portable typewriter. I was determined that being a mysterious bachelor and staying up late at night under a gooseneck lamp would be romantic. All right, I was still in love with my high school sweetie, but I knew better.

A few years later I had an MA and a wife. I had never really thought out my reasons for staying at university after that. But now here I was, and the normal order of things seemed to be to get a professor job, which I did by the skin of my teeth at the University of Alberta in Calgary. Every academic job I was ever to get would be by the skin of my teeth, as it turned out.

I had figured that I could be a full time writer if I were either rich or poor, so I could get a working job, or I could be a university teacher. I chose teaching as a more pleasant alternative to either starving or working. I could then define myself as a writer who teaches literature. That way, too, I could have more of a hand in organizing my time. As a university teacher you don't have to stack things or lug things, and you don't have to get up at seven every morning. I looked on it as a way of buying time to write.

So I taught for three years at Calgary, then did a year as a PhD student at the University of Western Ontario, then hired on as writer-in-residence and eventually as a teacher at Sir George Williams University in Montréal, then came to Simon Fraser University on the west coast. I did a sabbatical semester from time to time in Europe. And everywhere I went I kept on writing, kept a schedule of writing, but I never skimped on the academic job — I gave and marked more assignments than my colleagues did, and I published as many literary and critical essays and reviews as any of them did. I didn't want them looking down their noses at a mere novelist amongst them.

As you can imagine, a person has to have some kind of self-discipline to live these two work lives. Especially if, as in Calgary, he is also the caretaker of the apartment block in which he is renting an apartment, because he's getting only $5,000 a year from the university. Even more so if he also has to carry on a career as a ballplayer and a sports journalist for underground newspapers. So I got into a routine, and that routine saved time, and the deadlines got met.

I am not good at writing on the run, unless I set up a project, such as a novel, that is designed to be written on the run. But that is another story that I'll get to later. I am the opposite in this way from Allen Ginsberg, who could write poems in his notebooks while riding in the front passenger seat of a car. If I get so much as a telephone call during my writing time the day will most likely be shot. The older I get the more time I take off for such flimsy reasons.

There have been variations in these routines over the years, depending on whether I am in a hotel in Trieste or marking a hundred term papers, but a few things have been pretty constant. I usually write in the afternoon and early evening. My desk is a mess, but I can find just about everything on it I need. I decide early in a project or shorter piece whether I will write the first draft by hand or on a keyboard. I am a little obsessive about reading and writing. I have scribblers listing the titles of every book I have read since I was fourteen. My diary is almost fifty years old, and it is written in single pages in a series of black stiff-covered exercise books.

Now that I am retired I do not have many university hassles left to deal with, so I have only one full-time job. I have a daily routine on days I don't spend in airplanes and hotels. First I get up kind of late, sometime between 9:15 and 10:45, do teeth and eyedrops, then put on my housecoat and slippers and head downstairs. There I make coffee and read the newspaper, scowl at the box scores, do the *New York Times* crossword, have another coffee, and read three chapters of the Bible.

But then there is more avoidance to indulge in upstairs in my computer room. First I have to read my e-mail, and if it is Tuesday, study my week's results from the organizers of my fantasy baseball league. In the winter, during the non-baseball months, I prepare for the next season. Sometimes the e-mail tells me that I have to do something writerly at once, such as reading proof for a story coming out in a magazine very shortly. But eventually, well — there is the keyboard right there, with no more pencils to sharpen, no more bookshelves to alphabetize. And that's where the self-discipline kicks in — I don't do my exercises and shower until I have made some progress at my desk.

While writing my prose books, novels or histories or whatever, I have always kept a daily word count. For the longest time it was four pages, which was somewhere over a thousand words. By my third history book, I was down to three pages a day. Nowadays I don't have a word count but I do have a rule — some increment every day, unless the World Series is on. But the most important thing about a routine is when you go to bed at night, you do so knowing that you've put some more words in that darned computer.

I mentioned that I write in the afternoons. It is 1:02 p.m. right now, for example. There was one time that was different. Upon returning to Vancouver in 1971, we joined a commune in an old house in Kitsilano. There were seven people living in that house, some workers, some students, two pregnant women, a gay couple. It was easy to work out the cooking schedule — seven people over seven days. Setting aside writing time was more complex. We had to accommodate job hours, and keep out of each other's hair. So I chose one in the morning 'til five in the morning. I was on a Canada Council grant, and would not have a job until later in the year. When I went to bed, the five in the morning person would take over. It was a productive routine.

### 3. *Writer as Father*

Angela and I were married for nine years before we had our one child, who is now the short story writer Thea Bowering. Her arrival coincided with our return to Vancouver, and my soon taking another job teaching, after a year of writing on a grant. So now I added childcare to teaching and the telephone as pressure on my writing time. Over the years I have heard women writers describe motherhood as a restriction on one's time for "creativity," a restriction that male writers allegedly do not experience. I feel the same way about this presumption as I feel about professors who regard my publishing record as not scholarly.

That is to say, I did more than my share of childcare, and if in those circumstances I did not manage four pages of text a day, I would still get *some* writing done. I just had to become more flexible in terms of my hours. I might not write in my diary every day. And sometimes at three a.m. some baby puke might end up on a manuscript.

I took my daughter to buy shoes — I liked that, except for the rapid escalation in shoe prices, and the frequency with which small female human beings change shoe sizes. I took her to daycare, Brownies, skating lessons. I learned to cook. I made school lunches — always drew faces on the bananas and hardboiled eggs. For years I put real cheese in celery and for years she threw it away because of my thumbprints. I took her to my ballgames and poetry readings. Now she's a grown-up ball-playing writer.

I fixed my teaching schedule so that I did really long days at SFU twice a week, to be available to my family as much as possible back on the west side of Vancouver. I didn't like those two four-hour night classes. It was a little tough to write seven days a week in those days.

But I'm not complaining. It is really neat to have a daughter, especially one who winds up spending some of her allowance on poetry books. And now it is really neat being the father of a writer.

I don't know what it is like for her, writing with the same last name as mine. It's a good thing my name isn't Atwood or Munro or Watson. But I like to read the stories Thea writes and see how damned good they are. She has invented her own method or form or something, and it is really interesting. She is a stylist, but does not "express herself" or all that other phony stuff. She has taken to writing as her niche in life. She's writing these long fictions, and writing for weeklies in Edmonton, and organizing reading series and so on. She's also supposed to be writing her Master's thesis. I remember when I was supposed to be writing mine. I always tell people that she's writing better stories at her age than I did. And sometimes I find in her work a sly dig at one of my stories or peccadilloes.

## 4. *Routines*

I like to have a spot for writing, so I don't write much on the plane, and I don't carry my laptop to the porch. I like the steadiness of a writing place. Remember Alice Munro's story about the housewife-writer who gets herself an office across town? Roy Miki and Daphne Marlatt have done that. The four years that I was in Montréal, although I had a writing room in our apartment in lower Westmount, five days a week I rode my one-speed bicycle downtown and worked in my windowless office at SGWU. I got my mail there. I had my typewriter there. While there might have been a gaggle of visitors at the apartment, I might be holed up in my office in the middle of Montréal.

Back in Vancouver I didn't do that. My university office was twenty-some kilometers away, and my one-speed bike had been stolen. So in our huge house in Kerrisdale I had a room to myself. I also eventually stole my kid's old toy room and ended up with two offices, across the hall from each other, both with bookshelves on all their walls. Now, here in West Point Grey in our smaller house, I still have my own writing room, with framed pictures of Shelley and Olson on the wall beside me.

I write in silence, except for the occasional passing fire truck, and the dog groaning in her sleep behind me. I sometimes say that I envy my painter friends, who have CBC radio going while they work. Robert Creeley used to play Charlie Parker records while he wrote poetry. The only time I remember creating sound in my room on purpose was when I was doing an experiment with automatic writing that Gertrude Stein had used in a graduate course.

Unless I decide to do a project that requires travel, I like to hole up around the same time every day to get back into the space I was in yesterday. I wrote one travel novel, *Harry's Fragments*, in Australia, Rome and Berlin, as the plot took place in those sites. On the other hand, I wrote another novel, *Burning Water*, in Trieste and Costa Rica, because I wanted to be away from the west coast, where the plot took place. I wrote a long poem, *Blonds on Bikes*, in Denmark, including a bit in Germany, because I was trying to write something like jazz riffs approaching the day's details of where I was. I wrote a long poem much earlier, called *Sitting in Mexico*, and so on. There are more. I wrote a long travel piece in 1966, when I took my typewriter with me for my first trip to Europe, across to Istanbul and back, two thousand words a day. I never published that, except for bits of it here and there.

I guess you could say that this writing elsewhere is a kind of regular thing in my life. Here is a thought, though: when I was in some foreign place, for example Trieste, it was easier to keep to a routine than it ever was at home. I didn't have a telephone, for one thing, and I wasn't getting mail, except the odd letter from home. In Trieste I would get up in the morning, have coffee and read the paper, *Il Piccolo*, then go for a very long walk and explore some site I hadn't seen before, thinking all the time about Captain Vancouver. I had been researching for a year and a half before coming to the Adriatic, and I had a Canada Council attaché case filled with index cards all sorted by subject. In the afternoon I would sit in my hotel room and handwrite one thousand words in the special Chinese hardcover notebooks with a ship design on them that I had bought for the purpose in Chinatown, Vancouver. In the early chapters I could do a thousand words in a couple of hours. In the last chapters it would take a ten-hour day to get a thousand words. It happens that way because there is so much to keep track of, in the end.

There are moments of anxiety while writing on the road however, as for example when my attaché case went missing on the Italian jet between Milan and Gorizia, or when I had to leave my manuscript in an unlocked cubicle in a cheap hotel in Costa Rica.

There's another good thing about writing in foreign cities. In Trieste or San Jose or, say, Piraeus, there really wasn't anyone I knew for thousands of miles around, so I could once again practise my solitude as well as my routine. I learned solitude when I was a boy, walking the hills around my hometown of Oliver, sometimes with my dog, or by spending hours in my room making a baseball game out of dice and booklets. I used the dividers in Shredded Wheat, semi-transparent linen writing paper, paste and the funny papers to make a set of collector cards, five cartoon characters to a card (the cards were as big as the Shredded Wheat dividers). The rule was that there would be five different strips represented on each card. I traced the funny papers at the window as we used to do. Such a card might, for instance, have the faces of Dick Tracy, Andy Gump, Little Orphan Annie, Major Hoople and Invisible Scarlet O'Neill on it. I wish I could find them now. They'll have been among the stuff my unsentimental mother chucked, I'd guess. I didn't know at the time that I was training myself to be a solitary writer.

The other side of solitariness, if that is the word, is loneliness, and I was lonely most of my life. But solitude is necessary, I think, to fiction writers, especially novelists. Maybe some novelists have to hang out with their characters, in the world they are making for them. As for my kind of novelist, for whom sentences are more important than characters? Maybe we need to be alone with our sentences — to *serve* them, to use the inevitable pun.

### 5. *Writing With Others*

The opposite of solitude is collaboration, which I have been practicing more and more in my later years. When I was younger I liked my solitude too well to work with other people. On occasions when people have staged or screened my few plays I have always said go ahead and do whatever you want, because I didn't think I wanted to collaborate with directors and actors and so on. But come to think of it, there were some early exceptions to the rule. In the *Tish* days we would sometimes rewrite each other's poems, and help each other rewrite them, as Coleridge tried to do with Wordsworth, and Pound did with Eliot and others. Frank Davey and I used to do twin poems on a given subject. But I did not do real collaboration 'til quite late, unless you count working with an editor.

Of course I have always liked collaborating with dead poets, and have got some of my best poems that way. And I have always collaborated with musicians. I wrote those youthful songs with my pal Will, and later wrote words for songs played by Gary Kramer and his rock group The Works. It was neat going to a dance and dancing to one's own stuff. I have co-written orchestral and choral music with professional composers, and even performed in a concert hall with Mario Bernardi. Recently I made a video with a jazz trio in Toronto.

I have sometimes heard people refer to groups of actors and musicians and so on as "families," but I wonder whether that makes sense, whether we are still talking on the subject of writing and family life here. That's funny, because I have done some collaborative work with family — with my late wife Angela. (I am not counting the story my daughter Thea wrote in reply to my story "Staircase Descended.") In one of my later books you will find a sequence of prose poems called "Pictures." There are ten pieces by Angela and ten pieces by me. It was her idea, I think, to choose five pictures each, from magazines, anywhere, and write pieces about them. I always thought that among her motivations for this task was psycho-analyzing me. It turned out really well.

We also collaborated with David Bromige and Mike Mat-thews on a four-person novel about our college days. We got the idea in a restaurant called Piccolo Mondo, so that became the title of the novel, which turned out to be a kind of sci-ence-fiction espionage campus comedy. It took a few years to complete because we had to keep waiting for Mike's chapters, which were always brilliantly funny.

More recently the young writer Ryan Knighton and I wrote a nifty book called *Cars*. We wrote fifty little prose pieces each, and they were published face to face, and then we did something more difficult for the middle two pages. This book has been filed as everything — poetry, memoir, fiction — it was even reviewed in the automotive pages of some southern newspaper.

I have often caught myself saying that all serious literature is part of a huge collaborative act. That is one of the reasons, I suppose, for my contention that there is no difference between reading and writing.

But that doesn't mean you have to get along with everyone in the family, does it?

*Working in an Erickson*

*I came back to the west coast and started teaching at* Simon Fraser University in 1971. I had wanted to work there because despite its recent shakedown of the Political Science, Sociology and Anthropology departments, the university had not quite yet learned how to be like all the rest of them — there were a lot of writers in the English department, some of them good.

It was a kick to have an office in Arthur Erickson's huge academic quadrangle, because it was so much unlike the places I had been just before that — Calgary, Western Ontario, and Sir George Williams in Montréal. Living in an Erickson: that big square outline made of concrete, with forest or mountains on the outside, tamed vegetation inside, along with its architect's trademark reflecting pool and pseudo-sacrificial hill. For the first ten years I had a view of the inside, and for the other nineteen years I had a view of an inlet and some mountains on the outside. There was not a lot of smog. You had to pile books on the air intakes, because someone always had the heat pumped up.

I know that there will always be businessmen who want to make amendments to Erickson's ideas, and his idealizations get chipped and cracked a lot. The worst example of this I have seen is in Lethbridge. There is a soft *arête* overlooking the city, and the architect built the University of Lethbridge so that it would take its harmonic place along that horizon. Then some cretin developer raised a highrise between town and gown. The only way to fix that mess would be to tear it down.

I have heard from people who would like to do that to Simon Fraser University, if you want to know the truth. Two famous Jewish-Canadian writers from Montréal opined that it looked as if it could have been commissioned by Hitler or Mussolini. Well, they were both associated for a while with Sir George U., a fourteen-storey arts building surrounded by delicatessens. I have to admit, though, that one winter day in my last year of teaching at SFU, I was standing outside a northwest door of the quadrangle, smoking a cigarette I had found, impelled to stay in one place for five minutes. All I could see on all sides, it seemed, was rain on concrete. Not a tile in sight. Thoroughly depressed, I was longing for bamboo.

I think that Erickson's SFU is for looking from rather than looking at.

All the way 'round the square on the inside there was a wide balcony off the sixth floor. You could not step out onto it from any of its many hallway doors because these were nailed shut. But you could get onto it from a professor's office or from one of the washrooms. I once walked all the way 'round, avoiding bits of erosion and other rubble and the higher weeds growing from the cracks. Some department secretaries had set up bird-feeders on the balcony. A few of them put out chairs for lunch and suntanning. But usually you could walk the whole way 'round without seeing anyone else. In later years when smoking was banned inside the building you would see thousands of cigarette butts on that balcony along with the empty packages they'd come from. I am usually pretty good at knowing my directions. Even in that windowless Sir George Williams building in Montréal I knew where north was, even though the Montréalers were themselves pretty fictive about that. But in the academic quadrangle at Simon Fraser University I did not teach the work of Samuel T. Coleridge because, as you remember, he saw the poetic act as making "the external internal, the internal external." For about fifteen or twenty years I kept being surprised when I came downstairs and went out onto the grass — surprised that I was not on another side of the lawn. It was also a little confusing to be walking westward (I think) along the third floor north concourse (which was the ninth floor if you looked at it from a few paces north in the classroom complex [what a neat name!]) and where you could see a flight of steps complete with gorgeous big shiny wooden banisters leading up to a concrete block wall with no doorway.

I took that to be Mr. Erickson's whimsy, a little suggestion that he too could find room for a little Dada in among his regular Modernism.

# May I Bring You Some Tea?

## Introduction to

### THE HEART DOES BREAK

*Winter is come and gone,*
*But grief returns with the evolving year.*

— P. B. SHELLEY

*Every year, as September gives way to October,* my wife Jean Baird feels a bleakness that comes with deep loss. She wanders a little, tears in her eyes that make it impossible to handle sewing needle or keyboard. She sometimes gives way to sobbing when she needs to be alone, and she has to have someone with her as autumn makes its way.

In the morning of October 3, 2006 we were wakened by the bedroom telephone in our home in Vancouver. The dread that one often feels at such a moment multiplied as I saw the emptiness in my beloved's face. I knew what it was about. Jean was shaking, sitting up in bed, the telephone in her trembling hand. She said "It is just not getting through to my brain," and I knew for sure. I held her, feeling necessary and useless. We humans are forced to hear the worst things possible.

Jean's daughter Bronwyn, twenty-three years old, was dead in a car crash in southern Ontario. Her aunt Jane, Jean's best friend, had to identify her niece from a photograph the police had shown her, and then telephone Jean.

While I hurried to the travel agent to buy plane tickets, Bronwyn's brother Sebastian went to his high school and Jean spent more time on the telephone. Then while I went to the school to bring Sebastian home, Jean cleaned up the kitchen and read her e-mail. We were all crazy.

Jean was acting just too ordinary. I waited for her to scream or fall on the floor. Sebastian at least put his fist through a wall. "I don't know what I should do," she kept saying. I thought about Middle Eastern women who are photographed wailing and clutching at air when a family member gets killed. Over the next few days Jean said such calm things as how fortunate it had been that it was not a two-car accident. A few times she disagreed with the sentiment that the loss of a child is the worst possible bereavement. In her work she had encountered people in lifetime comas following brain injuries, other people reduced to immobility. But how could she imagine that anything was worse than this? I thought that she must be in that famous denial, but I worried, I loved her so. I'd thought that crazy meant berserk. But now I know that the serene Mary in Michelangelo's famous Pieta is completely mad.

Over the following year Jean had to have the sanest head and strongest heart in the world to survive the idiotic things that people said to her in the way of commiseration. You have another child? Oh, good. Then it isn't so bad. You must be very happy to know that Bronwyn is with Jesus in Heaven. Time will heal your pain. You should start living your normal life again. I know exactly how you feel. When a new soul comes into the world it has already chosen a day for leaving it; you have to accept her decision.

Some of these wise thoughts and others just as sapient came from family members.

I sometimes feel that I should describe the terrible treatment of this woman by people who should have been trying to help her. But I want to respect her privacy, and give her a refuge in a time when solace is not possible, because I also remember that she was treated well by her longtime friends in Port Colborne, Ontario, and by the young people who were Bronwyn's good friends. These young folks allowed her to give to them, a true exchange, because their loving mournfulness sustained her for that first week in a world that threatened to be empty. It was Thanksgiving week, and meaningfully so as friends her own age gave her food and a place to sleep and a car for her husband to drive about the Niagara region. You may imagine how precious those things were that week.

When the strange ordinariness was over and Jean did manage to break down, her best friends just let her. Just let her. They did not cajole or demand, as the stupid will, that she "pull herself together." Sebastian needed time with his and his sister's old Port Colborne friends, and we did not have to know what he was doing day and night, only to hear his voice on his cell phone from time to time.

And sure enough, as a year passed, and then a second year, the bereft mother did not "get over it." Sometimes the horror came unexpectedly, and Jean needed some time to suffer, and maybe a hand to hold. When the earth finished an orbit, and October 3 was approaching, Jean felt the sorrow and lonesomeness and compassion for her daughter almost overcoming her. The time of year does that to you. It is not a year later; it is that day again. Grief returns with the evolving year, indeed.

2

*Well, every one can master a grief but he that has it.*

— WILLIAM SHAKESPEARE,

*Much Ado About Nothing*

Jean Baird's approach to any problem or project is to get a lot of books and read. When she perceived a problem with the literary awards syndrome, she began reading all the short-listed books for every year's Booker Prize. When someone close to her admitted to an eating disorder, Jean researched the subject thoroughly, even reading all the information to be found in hospital libraries. She hoped that her way out of the craziness after her daughter's sudden death was to be found, if it existed at all, in books.

Jean has been around books all her life, and not only as a reader. She was co-editor of a magazine about brain injuries, and later publisher of a magazine for young writers and artists. She worked for the Canadian Writers' Trust, and managed Canada Book Week. She began and organized the project to mandate Canadian texts in British Columbia high school English curriculums. She invented the Al Purdy A-Frame Trust to save the late author's house from the bulldozers.

Jean earned her PhD with a literary bibliography. She knows research. So for a year after that devastating morning she read dozens of books about bereavement. For a while she attended meetings of a helpful group called Compassionate Friends. There a circle of parents who had lost their children a year ago or a decade ago told one another their stories. In their meeting room at a church in North Vancouver they had a big box filled with books you could borrow. Jean borrowed some of these and donated others to it.

Some of the books were self-published poems. Most of them were like the ones that Jean had found in bookstores and libraries and the Internet. There were volumes written by psychiatrists, psychologists, journalists, gurus, preachers, television stars, medical doctors and trendy therapists. Many of their authors felt that they should have letters after their names on the covers of their books. Grief "resources" are all over the Internet. They include PowerPoint™ treatments! Jean read a lot of these books and parts of a lot more. She found one that offered the same twelve steps that are supposed to cure people of kleptomania or stuttering. Some of the people in the "helping professions" think that readers can "get over" their grief, or normalize their lives, or find a purpose in a world that seems to have become beyond comprehension.

It did not take a year for Jean to discover that the really helpful books were those written by real writers rather than self-help mentors. Dora Fitzgerald, a therapist and friend who lives on Galiano Island, listened to Jean's questions and gave her a copy of Joan Didion's *The Year of Magical Thinking*, arguably the most famous grief narrative in recent times. In 2003, a few weeks after Didion's daughter lapsed into a coma, her husband the novelist John Gregory Dunne died at their dinner table. The book both narrates the dreadful details of suffering its author faced, and describes the operating principles of grief and mourning. Didion has always been celebrated as a stylist. Here she never romanticizes a life of relentless shocks, offering a reality no twelve-step program could ever approach.

Another marvelous California woman is Isabel Allende,

who wrote a similar story. Allende's daughter, while living in Spain, was attacked by porphyria, a dreadful blood disease, and fell into a coma from which she would never awaken. Allende and her son-in-law brought the comatose woman to Allende's home in California, where the mother began to tell the story of her life in South America and Lebanon to her sleeping daughter. The result was the supernal memoir *Paula*.

Another therapist and friend, Karen Tallman, who had lost her own son in a dreadful accident, and who had grown up with parents who were experts in both the literary world and the therapy world, took Jean to Banyen Books and showed her which writers about mourning were the best. One was Thomas Lynch, a successful poet and essayist who lives in Milford, Michigan. He is also the third-generation director of Lynch & Sons funeral home, and the author of two books about life as an undertaker, *The Undertaking* and *Bodies in Motion and at Rest*. He was the subject of a 2007 PBS television special and the inspiration for the serio-comic HBO series *Six Feet Under*.

A village undertaker is a different thing than a cosmic energy maven. The human beings that come through Lynch's place of work are people he knew in life, and he will see their families in town. He is not going to be on late-night TV, telling you to get out your credit card. As a writer, he takes the care you expect from your hometown friend. So he says at the end of "Local Heroes," his poem about the aftermath of Hurricane Katrina's destruction of New Orleans:

> But here the brave men and women pick the pieces
>    up.
> They serve the living tending to the dead.

They bring them home, the missing and adrift,
They give them back to let them go again.
Like politics, all funerals are local.

It may seem strange that a woman seeking some sense in a world from which her daughter has been taken would turn to stories about the handling of dead people. But the words written by a writer rather than someone looking for a "client" saved my wife's spirit.

Although Jean has spent a good part of her life reading and promoting Canadian writing, during her first year of grieving her own daughter she found no Canadian narrative on the subject, none that can reach one's soul, or is it spirit? Jean will always be grateful to Karen Tallman for introducing her to Katherine Ashenburg's *The Mourner's Dance*. After her daughter Hannah lost her fiancé to a car crash, Ashenburg began to research the varieties of human mourning and to think about a book to be subtitled simply *What We Do When People Die*. Thus for Jean Baird the reader, Ashenburg's book was a godsend — or at least a lucksend. Finding out the ways in which human beings have learned to live with mortality and inevitable horror meant that Jean knew that there were better ways to live than some of those that had been visited upon her. And the reason for this solace was the quality of Ashenburg's writing.

In 2008, after the work on our anthology had begun, Abigail Carter's *The Alchemy of Loss* told the first-person story of a wife and mother whose husband had telephoned her from the stricken World Trade Center, and never came home. It is a memoir of five years during which the expatriate Canadian lived through both her family's grief and the public USA tragedy. The writing is done by a first-time author, but the words are plainly felt and honestly depict the promised "alchemy" that transformed Carter's "loneliness and isolation" into highly readable narrative. It is the kind of book that both Jean Baird and Abigail Carter wished had been there for them while the world was crazy.

3

*I will teach you my townspeople*
*how to perform a funeral*
*for you have it over a troop*
*of artists —*
*unless one should scour the world —*
*you have the ground sense necessary.*

— WILLIAM CARLOS WILLIAMS, "Tract"

Jean always has a number of projects under way, so I was not surprised when she decided to look for some Canadian writing about grief and mourning. We are a country of poets, so it was not hard to find good poems about loss, such as Dennis Lee's *The Death of Harold Ladoo*, or good novels such as Matt Cohen's *Last Seen*. There are also scads of tributes to the departed, memoirs in verse and prose, fictive and less so. We did find a few excellent non-fiction pieces, and will recommend reading, for example, Patrick Lane's two pieces about losing his mother — see his book of mixed verse and prose *Go Leaving Strange*.

But the editors and publishers of what became *The Heart Does Break* were looking for new material, commissioned stories rather than reprinted ones. There were writers that we coveted for the project shamelessly who said that they could not, for various reasons, approach the subject. There were others who said that they were too busy writing or publicizing a novel. There were some who almost wrote a story for us, and others who almost didn't.

The variety of stories that did arrive on our desks reminded us again of something we had learned over the past couple of years — there is no limit to the number of ways in which grief occurs or in which human beings mourn. Katherine Ashenburg's book describes some of the many ways in which differing cultures perform a funeral. Our stories tell us that individuals, too, are various in their mourning.

A lot of people are ill at ease around someone who is in extreme grief. They don't know what to say or they say something stupid. They want to say something that will help the person "get over" it. But a grieving person does not want to get over it. Mourning is love for the one so sadly gone. "While grief is fresh," said Dr. Johnson, "every attempt to divert only irritates." If you want to say something to a widower or mother or brother, say it simply: "I am sorry for your loss. May I bring you some tea?"

4

*As long as skies are blue, and fields are green,*
*Evening must usher night, night urge the morrow,*
*Month follow month with woe, and year wake year to*
   *sorrow.*
                                   — P. B. SHELLEY, *Adonaïs*

The word "grief" has an old family. Its Sanskrit ancestor was *gurús*, and it showed up in Medieval Latin as *gravis* and Gothic as *kaurus*. From the beginning it has meant heavy. Curiously, Medieval Latin has the form *gravidus*, signifying heavy with child. What a grave attitude the Europeans had of our mortality back then!

But in the heaviness that joins the grave to the womb, there is a reason to write an elegy — that poem that begins by relentlessly immersing us in sorrow, but then, after a long wait, tells us about birth, or rebirth. In Shelley's poem the departed John Keats takes his place among the stars, "the abode where the Eternal are." Next time you go to a wake, see the way the adults act around the newest baby or the most pregnant mother in the family. They gravitate, perhaps. Check Linda McNutt's story in this collection.

Grief is the weight we feel, the gravity that orders us when loved ones die, even as we know that they must, even as we still hold an unspoken hope that the next one never will have to accede to the general rule. Grief is what finds us, mortals that we be. Mourning is what we learn to do. William Carlos Williams told us that we are called on to perform a funeral, and so we do, mourning not something given to us as grief is, but a challenge. It is the true subject of all the stories in *The Heart Does Break*.

The word "mourning" derives from the Old English *murnan*, which is from the Sanskrit term for both memory and anxiety, an interesting doubleness. Perhaps that says something about the sense we have of our own mortality while we are engaged in commemorating someone's life, or in solemnly attending a memorial. Maybe that is why we now talk about "celebrating" the subject's life rather than memorializing it. A century or so ago, Europeans and North Americans experienced a lot more family deaths during their lifetimes than they do now. Now the ubiquity of death is filtered through television screens, statistics and abstractions between us and Middle Eastern wars and African famines.

To be anxious. To grieve. To perform our love and respect. That is mourning. Sometimes, as you can see, writing itself can be an act of mourning. Despite the given procedures, mourning is not easy. The heart does break. At my father's graveside ceremony I was shocked to observe myself rushing from my Protestant family formation to kiss his coffin. So we find ourselves reenacting stories told by our forebears. When my first wife Angela died before the eyes of her daughter and me, I tried to close her eyes that had gone empty, and they would not, as they always will do in movies and novels, close. But one does at times of our most focused insanity desire to perform the olden story, properly to mourn.

5

*The day breaks not, it is my heart.*

— JOHN DONNE, "Daybreak"

Another way to mourn is to tell the personal tale, not to eulogize the departed mortal, but to narrate the survivor's story.

Sometimes it can be a depiction of solitude. All the while that the Newfoundland novelist Bernice Morgan was in the hospital attending her dying husband, the rest of the world was experiencing the destruction of New York's twin towers and the chaotic television screens of the days afterward.

At the Woody Point, Newfoundland writers' and musicians' festival, we went to hear Bernice Morgan read (and if you get a chance to do that, don't let it slip by) and naturally asked her to contribute to our book. Eventually we received a beautiful handwritten letter from her, telling us that she had come to the conclusion that she could not write about the grief she has felt since her husband George had died. Then with the help of

# 40 *Words, Words, Words*

her daughter, she had come to realize that much of what she had felt found its way into her novel *Cloud of Bone*.

It is a peculiar and delicate act, asking a writer to narrate his or her days or years of loss. A man who has garnered a lot of awards for his work told us that he is "without words" to deal with the death of a family member. A novelist whose grandson had been killed by an unrepentant driver put the question to her family and told us that they could not bear to see their story in print.

As we would hear many times, there are many ways to mourn, and some of them will not allow for written words at all. Some of our writers found the words slow and elusive, and had to rewrite and revise, in a way to piece through their re-enactment of the process. A few managed to be theoretical. Some viewed their own responses and behaviour with humour of various. Others followed their memories right down into the frightening hole behind the broken heart. Bill Whitehead's story of life after Timothy Findley continues to amaze me with its depiction of both despair and laughter — a reminder that in the theatre tragedy and comedy need one another to continue, and that we live and die in a theatre.

So yes, some people, even some highly successful writers, cannot write their grief, while others can tell about their being in the world that a loved one has left.

Just about everyone in our society wants to write a goodbye poem to their dead — just look at the obituary notices in the classifieds. But why would one want to write about being left behind? I think that your father's death, your daughter's, your best friend's death means that you are another person now. You need to be redefined. For one kind of person that might mean quitting your job and heading to Africa. For a writer it probably means writing.

For Jean Baird and me it meant editing the first Canadian anthology of that writing. Some of its readers have been people who are mourning a person who had defined their lives. The human touch, the art of such a thing, was our reason for collecting and offering those twenty stories.

*They are there like breath, instantly when something, anything, touches us.*

— RUDY WIEBE

*On bpnichol*

# On First Opening Nichol's Chaucer

CANTERBURY TALES, *it's a long poem that incorpor-*ates — that's a good word, with the gross corp, the body in it, the fart wheel, the big peckers and pants full of shit or a lusty woman with a gap between her front teeth, the church on one horse, the bawd on another — and I remember that Anselm Hollo in 1966, a year before bp started on his lifetime's epic, wrote naughty words in the gleaming pigeon poop on a bridge in Hyde Park, poetry gone contrary on the whited sepulchre.

So also does Charles Olson's own pilgrimage, celebrating or detailing a Massachusetts fishing town older than US-American history — lately filled with Italians instead of Adamses — make the most recent great Amerk poem, out of the narrative of a giant smoking man's breath, necessarily oppositional, a form of love that "is form, and cannot be without / important substance," one substance being the "gurry of it" that the speaker, so we have been taught to call him, is covered with, so that this big human mammal boasts the holes in his clothes, "my fly / gaping, me out / at the elbows" — the funniest misdirection in midcentury poetry, but is it really

45

misdirecting? Someone he purports to be quoting says that in
the face of sweetness a poet should

>    piss
>    and go
>    sing,

thus going "contrary."

    This is a hundred years, isn't it, after Emily Dickinson of
Massachusetts said to tell it slant, the truth.

    T.S. Eliot, who knew something about a long poem, did
not omit the smellier parts of human anatomy — it was just
that he assigned them to the lesser among us mortals. Modernism, his kind, called for education and taste, those things
that the cloacal James Joyce was often accused of lacking but
which he was actually rather forgoing. In his poetry, however,
he is all dews and dawns, and his verses are tiny pale-skinned
creatures, hardly longer than a sigh.

    When I read the first volume of *The Martyrology*, when-
ever that was, half a life ago, I had been told that this was a
poem written as a book, this was a book — yet I looked in
vain for what you'd grown used to finding up front in a book,
a page, after you'd turned some stuffing but before you'd got
to the meat, on the verso side, filled with information about
the coming into print of what is immediately to follow. Not
there: all we got was a kind of colophon at the end, letting us
know that Jerry Ofo had illustrated and printed this volume,
and that Coach House Press claimed to have run a thousand
copies in "early spring 1972."

    Okay, no — what *is* that page called? — but one's troubles
had only begun. As someone else has pointed out, we had to
give up hope of seeing bp knuckle down and start the poem.

There are, I don't know, twelve pages of *prefatory* stuff before we get to the title page, all of them suggesting that the book may have begun. We know that it is the title page, I think, because at the bottom, inside Jerry Ofo's border, it says:

The Coach House Press                    Toronto

But that's not my topic. It's fart wheels and pissing poets, and this stuff in Nichol's long poem far before we get to *Organ Music* — which I could have sworn was in-corporated, the way *Scraptures* were.

In Gertude Stein's plays the saints never move, because they aren't really supposed to have bodies. Well, Stein is the first person Nichol quotes, but that's, maybe, before the book starts; "so many bad beginnings," the *Martyrology* begins.

In our legal-psychological system we make allowances for bad beginnings. But what about our literary system? How many beginnings can a poet get away with? Eliot said that in our beginning is our end, or was it the other way 'round? He was nostalgic for the ideal. He was careful when it came time to piss. There was a lotus in that pond.

Just after the *Martyrology*'s dedication page, which is inside the poem, we're instructed:

the breath lies


on mornings like this
you gotta be careful
which way you piss


In the face of sweetness, I assume. Here is a poem begun in 1967, a centennial project, as one might have said, a hundred years after they started a serial country called ca-na-da, but a handful of years since *The Maximus Poems* was first published and became the presiding long poem in the New World.

Not that bpNichol was engaging in a pissing contest. Olson played the role of a large unkempt legend; bp was more likely to break into a Fred Astaire song, and sing it worse than Astaire did.

And for this low postmodernist no blow was too low:

december 67

the undated poem is
found and
            forgotten
                    passes
    like gas

Another bad beginning — or a saintly poem that starts with pissing and farting? A warning that no matter how touched you may be by the prayers to follow, form comes into being when the thing is born, and you should never give up having some damned fun with the fundament — it's like *ABC*, where nothing is sacred, and so is everything else.

# The Brothers Nichol

*If Captain Poetry didn't exist, someone would have to* invent him. That, come to think of it, would have been terrifically interesting to a kid such as I was. We comic-book-reading kids really liked the origin pieces — the origin of Superman, the origin of Plastic Man, etc. Those origin stories were the only thing that reminded us of the difference between the gods and the superheroes. As far as we humanoids were concerned, Apollo was there before any of our ancestors were, but a superhero (or a supervillain) can be created in an atomic laboratory accident.

I don't know what kids fall in love with these days. On the bus people are wearing white wires and staring at screens instead of looking at pages. I suppose that some kind of machine-gun-toting guy blasting away at furtive enemies takes up the attention of boys with nimble thumbs and little displays. Barry Nichol and I grew up in a world in which books were normal, and comic books were fascinating. Comic books led to poetry books for me. The first book of poems I ever bought came from the book and magazine rack at Frank's pool hall, where I habitually bought the new issue of *Detective Comics.*

An awful lot of superheroes, at least the male ones, attained the rank of captain. Terry Lee and Steve Canyon made it to colonel, eventually, but we generally had to rely on captains to save us from crooks and catastrophes. There were Captain Marvel, Captain America, Captain Midnight, Captain Atom, Captain Tootsie (the candy ad in the form of a coloured comic strip), even an Aussie named Captain Boomerang. There was something about a captain. An eleven-year-old kid didn't have any time for a major or a lieutenant-general.

Same thing for poets. "O captain! My captain!" "I am the master of my fate, / I am the captain of my soul." In *Captain Sword and Captain Pen*, Leigh Hunt takes up the latter instrument to battle the former. The Romantic poets kind of saw themselves as superheroes.

I am saying that bpNichol just would not leave childhood things behind. Poetry did not replace comics. Wanting to be a poet did not succeed wanting to fly. Not that bpNichol was necessarily Captain Poetry. When Michael Ondaatje titled his 1970 film *Sons of Captain Poetry*, he may have been thinking of Beep as one among them. And poems identified as coming from the pen of bpNichol are addressed to the mighty winged one.

I think that the first time I encountered Captain Poetry was in Nichol's magazine *Ganglia*, the third issue, published January 31, 1966, or more than a year before his first book, the box containing *Journeying and the Returns* plus a handful of textual things. The cover remains, forty-six years later, comically ambiguous. It is mostly made up of djNichol's drawing of Captain Poetry in typical comic book battle with a many-tentacled Ganglia. People who have seen Spiderman at it with Doctor Octopus know the scene. "In this issue," we comics fans are told, "the incredible Ganglia meets Captain Poetry."

On the contents page we get a shot of Captain Poetry flying, and then at the beginning of the mag's feature poem, Captain Poetry announces in a speech balloon: "I?! I am Captain Poetry! I have pledged my life to destroy thee Ganglia." My question is this: whose side do you think bp is on? Captain Poetry is figured as a threat to the magazine that positions the young Nichol in the Canadian poetry scene. Yet in dj's picture Ganglia looks like a threat and Cap looks like a typical costumed saviour of poetry. Remember that bpNichol traces his cultural ancestry to the Dadaists, who proclaimed often that they were about the destruction of art and the hoity-toity civilization it represents. No monuments for bp.

If you need persuading on this point, have a look at the three djNichol drawings at the beginning of *The Cosmic Chef*. This was bpNichol's anthology of concrete poetry published in 1970 by Oberon Press. The first shows a smiling, perspiring, shaky Captain Poetry holding on his back not a globe but a huge cube of concrete (get it?) that is showing cracks and bits of rubble falling off. On the front is chiselled in capital letters: "The Cosmic Chef / Glee & Perloo / Memorial Society [with most of the Y around the corner because dj ran out of room] / Under the Direction of / Captain Poetry / Presents . . ." The second picture shows the backside of the block, which is lying on top of Captain Poetry, parts of whom are visible, along with a few feathers in the air. On this face of the block is carved [in caps]: "An Evening / Of Concrete." Below the drawing: "Courtesy . . . / Oberon Cement Works." The dedication page, when you get to it, bears the names of five classic comic artists, and the third picture — a small pile of rubble and three feathers.

Or we could just have a good look at Captain Poetry. He is well muscled and appears to be without clothing, except for a bikini, two metallic things around his wrists, an anklet with attached heart-shaped locket, and the kind of monogoggle thing over his eyes that we have seen on blind superheroes. With his beak, he reminds us most of Hawkman, who was also fitted out with wings and a beak. But Captain Poetry has those worrisome wattles dangling where a chin might be expected. Sort of like Andy Panda's pal Charlie Chicken grown up. Hmm.

On the cover of his own book, Cap looks triumphant. Or is he just trying to shore up his own confidence? Is he someone we know, or is he the secret hidden from himself in someone we know? Listen:

> O he sings like a madman, talks like he's sane
> And does it each day again & again.

*Five Things I Know*

## 1. *The Romantics*

*People have noticed that while I claim some association* with innovative poets, one can find mention of the English Romantics in my poems. On my study wall I have a bunch of pictures, including to my right, two big portraits. These are of Charles Olson and Percy Bysshe Shelley. I know: that is odd. Before the summer of 1963 I resisted the Romantics, except for Blake, and that was only because everyone I knew was reading Blake, not just because Allen Ginsberg had mentioned him. Ezra Pound was not happy with the Romantics, nor the "sludge" that followed them, before the light of day finally provided by Hulme, etc. So of course I read Pound and the people Pound said we should read. My friends and I were reading "Donna mi Prega" or whatever and so on; but in the summer of 1963, during the big poetry bash in Vancouver, Allen Ginsberg, just back from Asia, recited Shelley's "Ode to the West Wind," and later *Adonaïs*, and so I was swept along.

I had expected to follow Olson all over for those three or four weeks of the '63 UBC poetry conference, but was surprised to find myself enjoying being in the orbit of Ginsberg.

Then I went to Calgary and taught for three years, and then
I went to London, Ontario, to be a graduate student, where
I took a course on the Romantics in which I paid most of my
attention to Shelley. As the years went by, most of the Romantics fanciers I knew were hot for Coleridge, but I persisted in
reading Shelley, even reading ten biographies of him. Eventually I went to Italy and checked out houses Shelley had lived
in, went to the Protestant graveyard in Rome, saw the grave
of Keats and took a leaf to give to my Keats friend in Vancouver, saw the "grave" of Shelley, etc. Yes, I do allude to Keats,
especially in my fourteen-page poem "Do Sink" that explodes
Keats's "cease to be" sonnet. I have also written a miniatur-
ized translation of Shelley's *Adonaïs*, something called "He is
Not." Etc.

It is more than true: innovative poets don't lean on the
Romantics much. Shelley, for example, rather than creating
new forms, decided to write the best poem going in every
verse form then known. I have for decades searched for a way
to combine the accuracy of Louis Zukofsky with the openness
to spiritual music of the Romantics. My search is ongoing.

I suppose that the most pleasing inspiration for such a thing
is Robert Duncan; and it so happens that of all the poets in the
Donald Allen anthology, Duncan was the one my friends and
I were most quickly and most closely connected with — my
generation of poets here in Vancouver: Fred Wah, Jamie Reid,
Frank Davey, Daphne Marlatt and David Bromige.

## 2. *Rules and happy accidents*

That anthology, *The New American Poetry*, had other inspira-
tions for me, too. A few years ago the young USAmerican
poet Al Filreis told me: "The main sequence for which *Blonds*

*on Bikes* is named reminds me very much of Kerouac's travelogue poems *Mexico City Blues*, though I'd give you the edge for assurance and maturity. Was this a planned resemblance or something that just happened? Following this, do you go in more for conscious craft or happy accidents? Has this changed over the years?"

I think he was the first person I know of who noticed this. That sequence *was* written with the Kerouac method in mind. Not *Mexico City Blues* in this case, but *San Francisco Blues*. I had made myself an extra rule, as I will do. That is, I had just one entry a day to make, trying to go as fast and unplanned as Jack did, whatever was there, something that worked because like him I was on foreign ground — in my case Denmark and Germany.

Of course, I was older than Kerouac was while he was writing his, and I had his space to piss in. So thanks, JK.

I guess I go for the happy accidents Filreis mentioned once I have set up rules — what I used to call baffles. I once wrote a novel the way I wrote that poem. It was a translation of the *Fragments* of Heraclitus. That is, I carried that book with me, and what I wrote each day (and I did not miss a day) had to use whatever was in the reading of Heraclitus that day, and what I had seen and done that day. *Harry's Fragments* takes place in Australia, Vancouver, Rome and Berlin. It also had to be a spy story, and it had to involve Thai restaurants, something not common in 1985. There were lots of happy accidents. For example, I arrived for chapter one in Sydney, Australia, the same day as did the *Queen Elizabeth II* and the SST — on St Valentine's Day.

The SST shows up later in Berlin. It happens that the day I got to Heraclitus's famous "The way up is the way down" was the day I first went to East Berlin. The East Germans had a

rule that said that you must leave East Berlin by the same way
that you entered: the S-Bahn, the U-Bahn, or Checkpoint
Charlie. The way in is the way out. A lot of those happy accidents happened — as they do in all my books, it seems.

I wrote a baseball fiction about the 1962 season in Vancouver, and I found that there was a UFO that chased people out
of the stadium one night in August. In an earlier book I chose
to write about 1888-89 in Kamloops, and had decided not to
mention baseball. But it turned out that there was a game on
New Year's Day, 1889, that was postponed by an eclipse of the
sun. What could I do?

## 3. *Progressively aging*

I never set out to write about the aging process, but there it
is, so of course you have to work with it or you will screw up
whatever it is you are writing. I always noted, when I was a
young punk, that Hemingway's hero was about three or five
years younger than he was when he wrote the story or novel.
He did get at the aging process *per se*, though, in his later
books — *Across the River and Into the Trees*, for example.

I think that you might be creating a sense of progression as
you write your way along your timeline, but I don't know how
to say anything intelligent about it. Like most other people, I
imagine, I see recent work as better than older work, having
built on its practice. But once in a while you see an early piece
and wonder how you could have got that. Maybe at the time
you were afforded a glimpse into the future when you would
be writing better.

But really, one keeps *reading* as one gets older, and so crams more into one's head, as one gets more sensitive to human experience. You do not want to repeat yourself, so when you try something new, you might as well make that something better.

## 4. *Other writers*

Some of the few literary commentators that are still around have noticed that I can't seem to get along without the help of other writers. I steal their characters and put them into my own fictions. I rewrite Rilke's elegies and set them in my neighbourhood. I collaborate with Shelley and Milton. I write Robin Blaser's lectures into my long poem. I write books about my contemporaries. Then there is that occasional sequence of poems that shows up in all my collections.

I call them my tribute poems. Actually, they are arranged not in lines but in sentences that usually take up two lines on the page. I have been publishing them in a number of books, and there will be another group in my next. These are pieces I write when a writer dies or has a big birthday, and hence a commemorative anthology or issue of a magazine or the like is to be made. I have occasionally (ha ha) thought of someday doing a volume of them — maybe after my own death. But then I think well, no, the process is that they are ongoing, a thing that happens when you get older in the art. There are some objects of these tribute poems that are still alive — Leonard Cohen, Pat Lane, etc. These are real occasional poems, as the occasion really existed, and would have happened whether I contributed or not.

### 5. *Online versus print*

I am still a print fetishist, if that is the right and fair word. Lately, as requests come in, I have been publishing online, and though I have come to think that the medium of the web is not totally secondary to writing, I still favour print magazines. I know that the circulation of online poems is bound (ha ha) to be greater, but what about books? Books are marvelous objects, amazing machines, so portable. I read a book in the post office lineup, which I can't do with online stuff, because I threw away my cell phone. I have been using computers since they first became available to individuals — I hate to think how long that has been, but I noticed yesterday that I am still using a password a techie in Denmark gave to me in 1995. I loved the exposure of being featured online in *Jacket* magazine, yes. I guess it all depends. I think that my feeling about online mags is similar to my feeling about print magazines — the attraction lies in the company. Who are you with?

*McFadden's Bugs*

*Often, when you read the poetry of David McFadden,* you think about his everyday world. He mentions his family, his friends and neighbours, his childhood, Hamilton and Toronto, the people on the street, the streetcars, coffee shops, the movies he's seen recently, books he's been reading, a typewriter he has borrowed and from whom he borrowed it. What you are reading is a life's diary, you think, sometimes merry, at times wryly unhappy. You figure that the Victor Coleman who appears in McFadden's poems is the Victor Coleman you know, and you are glad to see him, think of saying hello, almost.

But something funny happens to normal places when David McFadden comes strolling into them. If a cruise ship sits diagonally at the corner of Yonge and Dundas, or apple trees become musical instruments — I'm not saying that these things have happened in a McFadden poem — but anyone reading his books should not *not* expect them. Or maybe one should. Maybe the surprise is a lot better deal than an answer to "what does it mean?"

Recently someone mentioned to me a McFadden poem with horses in it, and I was reminded of his famous and often-published longish poem about a cow swimming Lake Ontario (it has had two titles). I thought of writing an essay about the animals in McFadden's work, their ordinariness and the wildly unusual world they find themselves in. I know that McFadden admires D.H. Lawrence, and has had a lifetime of oscillating feelings about Lawrence's *Birds, Beasts and Flowers*. Unlike Lawrence, McFadden is a city boy, having grown up in grittily industrial Ontario. But like the boys in the elementary school textbooks from Ontario, he got to visit and imagine a family farm, with a silo and all.

Here is what I wanted to do. I would observe motifs that show up in McFadden's animal poems, and then concentrate on the ones about farm animals. Of course my most concentrated attention would be focused on "The Cow that Swam Lake Ontario." I have heard that once McFadden dressed in a cow suit and read the poem aloud in a Toronto bar. Apparently it was not really possible to make out what he was saying.

But as I looked through my McFadden books and jotted a menagerie, I noticed that among the dogs, pigs, cats, jellyfish and elephants, there were a lot of insects. A bug in my ear, for sure.

It is true that McFadden's most famous poetry book, *Gypsy Guitar* (1987) has a winged horse on the front cover and a rhinoceros on the back cover, and that the poems inside present us with a hippopotamus, a cat, lots of elephants, a lion, some dogs, a snake, a butcher, some animal dreams, a monkey, the aforementioned jellyfish, more elephants, some cattle, a shark, a bunch of nestlings, some hummingbirds, plus an entire zoo, and that in its hundred pages the only insect to appear is an inchworm, the very image of the diminutive, perhaps of the unimportant. And yet, is its purpose not to measure, and is measure not the purpose of poetry in the world?

In the history of poetry, practitioners have often turned to an insect for focus. Irony attends composition as the mere, the negligible creature serves to illustrate a piece of wisdom or discovery. In classical poetry the humble caterpillar goes into hiding until metamorphosis gives us the lovely butterfly — symbol of spirit in the Mediterranean, sexual rebirth in the Gulf of Mexico. The ancient poet hoped for metamorphosis and tried metaphor.

For centuries in England one was as likely to see fleas on a person as on a dog, and the flea found its way into nearly everyone's poetry. Shakespeare remarks on the bravery of a flea that eats breakfast on a lion's lip. John Donne, in his famous flea poem, argues that his female companion may as well come across because a flea has sucked blood from both of them, so their vital fluids were already mixed. William Blake said of his famous picture "The Ghost of a Flea" that fleas were inhabited by the souls of "bloodthirsty men."

Apparently Blake was not as frightened by flies. You'll remember his simple little poem:

Little fly,
Thy summer's play
My thoughtless hand
Has brushed away.

Am not I
A fly like thee?
Or art not thou
A man like me?

etc.

A century and a half later, Charles Olson hears a fly while he is writing a poem, lets the fly into his poem, rimes with it, and lets it end his concentration and finish the poem, proving Olson's poetic:

> I measure my song,
> measure the sources of my song,
> measure me, measure
> my forces
>
> (And I buzz
> as the bee does,
> who's missed
> the plum tree,
> and gone and got himself caught
> in my window
>
> And the whirring of whose wings
> blots out the rattle of
> my machine)

But wait, it's a bee that Olson heard, and after all these years I misremembered it as a fly. That's a measure of forgetfulness. And a lost opportunity to say something clever about Rilke.

You would expect young David McFadden, among all his budgies and rabbits, to avail himself of the lowly fly and all its poetic history. In his first full-sized book *Letters from the Earth to the Earth* (1969), the first one to show up is a "November Fly," which appears in the bedroom among strewn papers. We have no doubt that the young poet did encounter such an insect, a creature that one does not expect to encounter that late in the year in Ontario. McFadden makes no remark about fleeting time or minute human importance. The fly simply enters and remains in his "confusion" as he goes to the cellar to look at the dahlia bulbs that have already been put there to spend their winter indoors. This is a very minor poem, and maybe that is what a fly should provoke. But look now. Years later I open the book and the fly, which should have perished unlamented decades ago, clings to life.

This is a book stuffed with family and local snapshots (real ones), and the poems, as the young father suggests, are other versions of them. The next book was *Poems Worth Knowing* (1971), the publication of which, we read in its introduction, "puts a cap on the 60s" for its author. There's an enigmatic little poem in it called "Counting the Dead," in which the poet looks at the dangling fly paper and "its load of tiny corpses" swaying in "the indoor currents of summer." The poet then enigmatically wonders about the strange new pain in his arm. We are getting Blake's poem with less music and more image. That McFadden does not spell out his observation as Blake does his, tells us that McFadden has the advantage of having read Blake, and his responsibility of getting in touch with our sensibility that has read Buddhist texts as well as Western ones. The sparrow's fall and then some.

The slightly enigmatic but still, remember, young poet of the sixties was introducing a post-snapshot element that would grow to become a major effect of his writing, not to mention his personal conduct. Of course the latter we will not mention because it is not allowed to become the subject of literary discussion. It will be omitted from this piece, whatever it is.

I think that the main purpose in being enigmatic springs from the desire to induce a reader to share the work of composition. Unless, of course, the poet really is innocent — an attribute that McFadden would apply to his narrator in his travel books. We do know that young McFadden was drawn to the William Blake who reported seeing a fairy funeral in his back garden. For years we would enjoy McFadden being awed by everyday things and calm in the face of miracles. Remember the butterfly — gorgeous image of almost magical transformation, yet something that happens in the insect world every year? In *Poems Worth Knowing*, young McFadden notes that when the Rolling Stones played a free rock'n'roll show at Hyde Park, commemorating their recently deceased former guitarist Brian Jones, they released a jar of butterflies. He did not note that Mick Jagger read to the huge audience from Shelley's *Adonaïs*. Brian Jones was a year younger than McFadden, and just a year older than the John Keats who was elegized in Shelley's great poem. Shelley's poem, like all traditional elegies, first mourns its subject's death, then denies it, suggesting the birth of greater, perhaps everlasting, life. So Keats is assigned to that "abode where the Eternal are."

McFadden, in only one long page, notes the ephemerality of the butterflies, then says that all lives will end, including those of the earth and other planets. Instead of proposing some elevation to everlasting fame, McFadden presents Nature (Wordsworth's word, I guess) as a "spirit so intelligent" because it absorbs all intelligent life and proceeds. At the end of the poem there is no transcendence for mankind, but a reabsorption into "a harmonious community / joyful with scientific contemplation."

**Even McFadden's reflection seems pre-reflective.**
**But what about this? For eleven years, though writ-**

**ing poems about wonder, he
worked all night as a newspaper
proofreader. Getting it right.
Remember that.**

His first book with a "major" publisher was *Intense Pleasure* (1972). Fellow McClelland & Stewart author Al Purdy is
quoted on the front dust jacket flap: "I'm particularly pleased
to inhabit the same world as McFadden, even if he's crazy as
a bedbug." Blurbs are not usually the subject of literary discourse, but this one is interesting. Purdy, known for taking
the immediate world as his material and doing so in the vernacular, recognizes a similar method in the work of his fellow Ontario poet, but feels that he has to make mention of
his colleague's irregular forms of observation. For this purpose, I happily take note of the insect that Purdy compares
McFadden to.

*Intense Pleasure* is full of short poetic observations on animals, but only one insect appears. Remember the butterfly
poem in which everything in the universe is dying while
Nature (which would seem to be a word for the living) derives
further existence from the result? In "June Bug," a poet who
refers to himself as a mouse (thus potential prey) watches a
sparrow land on a june bug, which in its agony bellows like
an "elephant," until a cat chases away the bird and chews on
the june bug, while the bird cries from its perch in a tree. The
mouse lives to breathe another day, but only in a world where
beetles "roar" and sparrows "sob."

You should remember that McFadden refers to poetry and
perhaps survival in the title of a later book, *The Art of Darkness*
(1984). Replacing heart with art is a sad result of becoming an
artist, I suppose, the replacement that Wordsworth portrays

in "Tintern Abbey" and elsewhere. I don't think that there are any insects in this book, though there is a menagerie of lions, armadillos, rats and so on.

1975's *A Knight in Dried Plums* has the odd bird in it, but no insects. The poems are getting longer as the poet matures, the social observations focus on human beings as examples of something, on relatives or newsmakers. McFadden is in his thirties, entering his period of prose narratives, the *Great Canadian Sonnet* volumes, the Great Lakes trip books, the stories in *Animal Spirits* and the novel *Canadian Sunset*. The collections of verse come out every few years, and there are some nice long poems published in chapbooks, but they don't have insects in them. It is as if McFadden has outgrown bugs. Did he do this to escape Purdy's low encomium? In his three M&S collections during this period, all we get in the ento-mological sphere is this one line in *Anonymity Suite* (1992): "Demons desert me like tricks a drowning dog," and to claim any "ticks" I have to accuse the professional proofreaders of missing a typo, knowing that you can't teach a drowning dog new tricks. Even if I get to claim them, the invisible ticks, they are deserting, or rather compared to something deserting the poet.

**Margaret Atwood's father studied insects for a living. I'll bet that *she* kept them coming in her poems of middle age. On the other hand, there are so many snakes in her poems, that maybe the insects have been thinned out. I will bet on wasps or yellowjackets, though.**

Most of the poets who published with M&S left for more poetry-friendly presses in the 1980s and 1990s. McFadden went to Talonbooks with editor Karl Siegler and then to some Toronto presses with editor Stuart Ross. As I have said, his first Talon book *Gypsy Guitar* boasts only an inchworm to inhabit our garden. You know that inchworms turn not into bright butterflies but into lacy geometer moths. According to their name, these small creatures measure the earth. Insect poets, one is tempted to say.

McFadden's second Talon book was needlessly titled *There'll be Another* (1995), and though it contains dead beluga whales, there are no insects.

> **But while reading it, pen poised, I thought about what a nice way it is to spend a day — reading David McFadden's poems. And this, after all these years: how deeply impressed one is by the substantiality of his work as it mounts up.**

When McFadden's third Talon book *Five Star Planet* (2002) came out, he tagged it as the "third volume in the Terrafina trilogy." Like the other two, this one sports plenty of animals, but it offers us only one insect poem, this being a peculiar postscript to a rumination called "What Does it Mean?" After more than a page of prose paragraphs, we get three stars to denote a space, and then:

> The seven ages of the fruit fly:
> Hour 1: Eat up all the fruit.
> Hour 2: Fly around like mad.
> Hour 3: Rest on the wall but be ready to resume

Hour 2-like activities when a large mammal
comes into the room.
Hour 4: Rest on the wall and forget about large
mammals.
Hour 5: Fall to the floor.
Hour 6: Die.
Hour 7: Get swept up by a large mammal who
resolves to keep fruit in fridge henceforth.

The majority of the poem is a sequence of nine memories
having to do with the individual's consciousness of bits of
strangeness in the ordinary world, and his wondering about
the possibilities of sympathetic magic. We see in the kid
moments that might lead in maturity to either metaphysics or
philosophy as a personal custom.

**After some internal quarrel I
have to report that while I was
typing this a fruit fly landed on
my computer. People who have
been around will know that this
was a McFadden moment.**

The fruit fly, which was the life's study of one of Canada's
major thinkers, here takes on the enigmatic role, *vis-à-vis* the
poem, as the poet's declared arm pain did when he reportedly
observed a group of dead flies after *their* sixth hour. Here, we
ken, is Blake again; here again is the denial of elegy. We know
that the large mammal will fall off his own wall, that his five
star planet will fall into the sun's flame or freeze when its sun
flickers out. (You will remember that Robert Frost skipped
the insects and went straight to fire or ice.)

Since his Talon days, McFadden has published four poetry books back in Toronto. Two of them are the big collected short poems and the big collected long poems. The third is a book of 129 sonnets called *Be Calm, Honey* (2008). Two of those three words suggest bees to me, a natural mistake, I think, and even more forgivable when one notices that the sonnets, unlike the Talon poems, are stuffed with insects. Further, their variety suggests to this ear with a you-know-what in it, that the entomofauna are there to make a point. There are a few animals in this volume, a jellyfish for example, a pig. But just as we are told that the post-catastrophic planet will be home to insects alone, so the poet's world in his senior years will be crawling with bugs. Crawling and burrowing and flying.

The nice third sonnet lets us warm up slowly. It is home to lizards, songbirds and "insects," plural and undifferentiated. Then we are left until the 25th sonnet, which brings us a firefly. In the octave the poet avers that he dreamt himself a "simple firefly," lazing about in the summer night.

Now I want to give just a hint to the complexity of McFadden's late sonnets. In the 25th one, he refers in the fourth line (always a site of importance in a sonnet) to the ending of *Hannah and Her Sisters*, Woody Allen's 1986 filmic tribute to Ingmar Bergman's *Fanny and Alexander*. I am going to suggest that you go back and see the endings of both those films, Allen's about an annual Thanksgiving family gathering, Bergman's about an annual Christmas one. Look for the transient firefly outside Hannah's house, if you like, but pay attention to yet another movie referenced, as the film essayists say, something that happens twice to the Marx Brothers' ill-greeted (a Woody Allen obsession) masterpiece *Duck Soup*, in which Groucho plays the part of the appointed president of Fredonia, a guy named Firefly.

You do know how much David McFadden loves coincidence and other such foldings of time. A working title for *Duck Soup* was *Firecrackers*. Some of the comic routines in *Duck Soup* were adapted from the Marx Brothers radio show *Flywheel*. All right, there are fires and flies anywhere that there is decomposition and transcendence. But as we are on the subject of insects, it is interesting to note that another working title for the Marx Brothers movie was *Grasshoppers*.

I would unravel further, but this is not an essay on movies. I will just go to McFadden's sestet, where he argues that usual poet's line(s): "we live for a moment then we die / but when we die we become alive." Well, in this case the "blinking bug" becomes a "dragonfly," or rather "will conceivably" do so.

The iridescent dragonfly is considered by some people to be the most beautiful creature of the insect world, a figure that can zoom or hover, a four-winged little angel that shows up in art all over the world. But like a dragon, it has always been seen as sinister, too, especially in Europe.

Imagine, then, the mixed feelings for the boy poet of the 55th sonnet, who bicycled with his mouth open and swallowed a dragonfly. Yes, there are Asians who eat these critters, but they cook them, ceremoniously or not. Little McFadden, or at least the boy in this poem, the poem maintains, sensed a dragonfly's dying in his "tummy," and traded "spontaneity" for the "universe of footnotes." The swallowed dragon(fly) of the octave leads to a complexity of attitudes in the sestet, where things are supposed to be decided or generalized. For me, the most interesting change is that the singular pronouns of the sestet give way to the editorial (or is it the royal) first person plural in the octave. I have given up trying to summarize what happens in those six lines. We do know that the poet has to zoom and hover to observe the meaningful, but that its climactic realization comes in a reported remark by an unnamed mathematician whose poetic job is to run off, but who talks like a movie star who never chose his part over his personality. Hmm.

I am guessing that in some way we become what we eat. You do know that dragonflies bite their prey in half, that people thought them to have teeth, and so assigned them the order *odonata*.

> (Oh, no, I've just remembered that last week, while I was working on this stuff, McFadden sent me a photo of his big gleaming smile and the adjuration "Look at those beautiful teeth, eh?" Another McFadden moment. It is a different experience, trying to write an essay about his work.)

So think of the dragonfly when you get to the 34th sonnet, the one about torturing a cockroach. And, by the way, if you are a teacher or the like, you might like to take this poem as an example of a veteran poet's ability to weave great complexity out of straight language. The poor cockroach here has to join in the performance of a soppy Irish song while waiting either to die, or in the long run, to inherit the earth. He is a bug we are revolted by, but not many of us would attempt to dispatch him with music. *Odonata* McFadden here portrays himself as a poet with a sadistic streak, something he has often done during his years of writing.

The 41st sonnet's octave will offer an unlikely but non-threatening simile connecting the sun with a beluga whale. The sestet will present new and improved spider webs among the cedars and a disconcerting absence of mosquitoes in those webs. The poem ends with these two lines: "Not that I'm criticizing you, Mr. Sun, (but could it be a bit too hot for mosquitoes?)" There is a nice intersomething here with the fate of the cockroach seen above. It is driven to its fate when the poet turns on the toaster under which it had been hiding. In the later sonnet we find something I like — an amusing and unpropagandish poem about unease due to global warming. The mosquito is a good choice here, McFadden's reminder of his insects that live on a planet as canaries live in coal mines. Blake and Lawrence helped write this poem.

> **Little bug, who made thee?**
> **Doest thou know who made**
> **thee?**
> ...
> **Did He who made the lamb**
> **make thee?**

Yes, we know that most of those insect poems in the canon are about human beings, starting with poets. The 47th sonnet of *Be Calm, Honey* begins: "The person writing these lines is very little. / He literally is knee-high to a grasshopper." I like the writerly duplicity here. The poet admits straightaway that there is no New Criticism here, that you can forget about any Browningesque "speaker" of the poem. Let Eliot hide behind or inside Prufrock. McFadden offers full-frontal nakedness. But then he says something that is patently impossible, and we have no-one to trust. We go back to remembering that except for butterflies and dragonflies, maybe, we could do without insects, even though our memory of high school biology reminds us that if the bugs ever go, we'll have been long gone. Ask the apiarists how the food supply is going to continue if the decline in the honey bee population continues.

"The person writing these lines" says that he makes a little living "scratching witticisms on windowpanes." Or scratching out sonnets for a small press, where the most important news in the world stays news.

> **Oh, the temptations! Last night we watched the Mel Brooks film, speaking of movies, DEAD, AND LOVING IT, wherein Dr. Dracula's foil spends quality time catching and eating insects.**

Having reduced his self-image in size, McFadden lowers it in respect, entertaining the role of the lowly maggot, a future fly that we observe with disgust (unless we are among those exotic people who make them part of their dietary input). Maggots devour carrion, and worse than that, swarm all over dead things. We correct ourselves by saying that this act is part of Nature's great plan, but we also know that a dozen flies take little time to lay eggs that will in little time be millions of flies. We don't like flies much but we are revolted by maggots. Replace John Donne's fly with a maggot or two, and note your response to *that* image.

Maggots are the last insects, or pre-insects, to appear in *Be Calm, Honey* (despite the title, bees do not make an appearance in the book). We expect abasement, I think. McFadden sets about associating not himself but "us," comparing, then contrasting. (Curiously, in the two maggot sonnets, the word "theory" occurs, but I will leave that interesting fact for another reader to address.)

To begin the 77th sonnet's sestet, McFadden announces: "Basically we're a swarming mass of maggots." In the octave he had flipped a coin to show two sides of humanity, one beautiful and courageous, the other greedy and murderous. That's to stand back quite a step in viewing humankind's presence in history. It's a further step to see us all as maggots, to remove decision and intentionality, to regard us as carrion-feeding instinct, unaware of any future transformation. Even such a future is no sign of hope now. McFadden advises us that "Each imago's destined for assassination." He allows that humankind can conceive of the notion of evil but adds that it has never persuasively accounted for it. And so the sonnet ends, ironically. A sonnet, with its sestet finished, is the type of the closed system. But this one ends with not only indecision but also the unlikelihood of decision. Meanwhile the maggots munch.

In the 110th sonnet the maggots are here, there and everywhere, serving several functions. You might think that all maggots do is eradicate dead bodies, but they have been used in medicine, for example, being dumped into wounds in order to clean up the dead and discarded tissue that has accumulated. They also serve as fish bait, and as mentioned, food for humans.

In the 110th sonnet it appears that either the maggots or the poet must be confused. First we find a pretty simple metaphor constructed for us: "The earth's a grapefruit rotting in the sun." (All right, you could argue that simplicity is left behind when the sun, usually our planet's life source, contributes to its demise — unless, again, we consider rotting as compost and thus a contributor to new life — you see what I mean?)

"The maggots that infest it have been evolving," so there we are: humankind as these repulsive larvae.

Then we humans are contrasted unfavorably with the squirming little white things. As we head for our self-inflicted annihilation, a holy hermit predicts that we will be transfigured (and then this terrific ambiguity): "If maggots can get along how come we can't?" It is twice ambiguous. To "get along" can mean never to fight each other. "[H]ow come we can't" assumes that we can't, or suggests that we can, as in "why not?"

Finally, in the sestet the poet gets ready to throw in the towel, if you will forgive an out-of-place figure (all right, cliché). In the last reference to any insect life in his poetry to date, the poet proposes a laconic couplet: "Perhaps the human race is not the greatest. / Perhaps the maggots will exterminate us."

It strikes me, as I struggle not to come to a conclusion, that if you were to read David McFadden's insect poems in chronological order you would probably have a good sense of his growing maturity and complexity as a poet. From the beginning, it is true, his writing has exhibited a kind of duality that I have not encountered in my other contemporaries — he has never left his (pose of) cherubic innocence, while he has admitted from the beginning a diabolic (not in the funny sense) streak, a blend of despair and Meursault-like destructivity.

In looking at the insect world, or the world that we must share with insects, he has found the best images for his double vision. We don't like bugs around us much, but we know that they are necessary to our globe and likely to inhabit it when we are discarded DNA. As flies to wanton boys are we to David McFadden's verse.

*A Little Baseball*

# Kids and Coots at the Yard

*In the middle of the night last week I returned to my* bed from the usual break, and thought about Johnny Lindell's hat.

All through my school years Johnny Lindell was an outfielder for the New York Yankees, and during the season of my high school graduation he was a pitcher for the Pittsburgh Pirates.

A lot of ballplayers do something funny to their uniforms or caps. Billy Martin used to make a cross out of straight pins right under the letter or letters on the front of his cap. I never saw another ballplayer do what Johnny Lindell did to modify his ball cap. Until the recent hiphop infestation, all players would bend the peaks of their caps into an arc so as not to look dorky. Johnny Lindell was the only one who would bend the two sides of the peak of his cap into right angles, about three-quarters of an inch from the edge.

So that's what I did with my ball cap. You've seen the way a lot of hockey kids hitched one side of their jerseys so that they got caught up on the shorts in emulation of Wayne Gretzky? Well, Wayne Gretzky was an obvious superstar, the Great One. Johnny Lindell wasn't even an everyday star after he got out of the minor leagues. But even though I detested the Yankees, as any intellectual kid would, I fell for the way Johnny Lindell wore his hat. Somehow, maybe, it meant that he wasn't really a Yankee.

More than any other game, baseball makes a fan think of his boyhood, and in some cases about her girlhood. If you go to a ballgame at Vancouver's Nat Bailey Stadium, for instance, you'll see only about three-quarters of the crowd that's there. The invisible one-quarter is inside a lot of the grey or bald heads from whose ears hang no thin white cords.

We old coots recognize each other everywhere. When I see an old coot at a ball park in minor league Ohio, wearing an old cap, with or without a scorebook on his lap and a pen in hand, I know he's one of us. I've seen him in underpopulated wooden stands behind home plate in Bologna, Italy. In that restaurant capital of the world there is no ball park food. If you want the best hotdog on the globe, go to the baseball field on the hill overlooking Basel, Switzerland.

Baseball is overshadowed by other games in backward countries like Italy and Switzerland. But in Canada it is our national sport, isn't it?

I certainly remember growing up in Oliver, BC, where it was basketball from November 'til February, and baseball from March 'til October. We had no ice hockey because there was no ice, and no football because there was no money.

The Vancouver newspapers act as if the only sports are hockey and football. I have a standing wager that on July 31 the first page of the Vancouver *Sun* sports section will be devoted to the Vancouver Canucks, an ice hockey team that seldom plays after the regular season, even in a league in which almost all teams make the playoffs. In the past few decades sports equipment stores have been selling expensive

ice hockey gear to the mothers of west coast kids. That's why
west coast kids, like those four kids on the five-dollar bill, all
shoot right-handed.

We kids in Oliver rarely got to go down to the Coast, but
when we did the first place we wanted to visit was the White
Spot, to have one of those famous hamburgers with the triple-
O sauce that ran up the underside of your forearm.

White Spot was created by the genius son of a circus wheel-
of-fortune spinner who had moved to Vancouver from Min-
nesota. Young Nat Bailey started a hotdog business when he
was a teen, and opened his first White Spot drive-in at Granville and 67th in 1928, the year after Babe Ruth hit sixty home
runs.

Bailey had been downtown hawking newspapers when he
was twelve. By the time he was in his fifties he was a Mason, a
Rotarian, a Chamber of Commerce gent, and a baseball pion-
eer. A lot of baseball fans bought Nat's hotdogs and popcorn.
When Little League arrived in the fifties the drive-in man
was there to get the kids up and running.

Oh, and also in the fifties the man in the famous bow tie
bought the Pacific Coast League's AAA Oakland Oaks and
renamed them the Vancouver Mounties. He kept them alive
at Capilano Stadium, opened in 1951, until they left town in
the late sixties.

Bailey died a couple of days after the Pacific Coast League
returned to Vancouver in 1978. Now the team would be called
the Canadians, and wear shirts that looked a lot like the label
on a beer of the same name. That year Cap(ilano) Stadium
would have its name changed to Nat Bailey Stadium.

Every year someone will remind us that the Nat is "the
prettiest little ball park in organized baseball." They say
something like that about the city of Vancouver, too. But

spoilsports point out that if you took away the mountains and ocean you'd have Welland, Ontario. Yes, and if you took away Little Mountain and its trees that stand just beyond the right field fence, you might as well be in Stade Municipal in Quebec City — except for the haze of cigarette smoke.

Still, Vancouver does have a pretty area in which to play or watch baseball, even after the hole-digging and chain-fencing and construction around much of Riley Park of a few years ago. The nicest Little League diamond I have ever seen was ripped up to make room for the rich people's winter games a couple of years down the line. Some of the parking lot had to go too. That did not affect me directly — I have used a secret parking spot nearby for many years. I have been to Class A games all across the continent, and Vancouver's is the only park I have seen charging cash for a parking spot.

But I love being in Nat Bailey. In 1971 I played on this field during the year-ending tournament of the infamous Kosmik League's inaugural season. There was no professional ball team in Vancouver. Nat Bailey was still alive, but he did not come out for our games, as far as I know. By the third day of the tournament the October mud was up to all the catchers' chest protectors. After I had batted in the tying run in the bottom of the ninth, my team, the Granville Grange Zephyrs, was edged in extra innings in the championship game by the slick Teen Angels. The guy who is now the oldest teen disk jockey in the world was playing for them. Luckily for us Zeds, the fans declared us the real winners of the title because in their opinion the Teen Angels were not truly Kosmik — they had matching teeshirts, and their girlfriends sitting in the stands had been to the hairdresser.

That was a high time for counterculture baseball, but a low point for the stadium. There was no professional ball in town.

The left field fence had been taken down to make room for a soccer pitch. Soccer! The stadium had even been consigned to the Vancouver Art Gallery, and weird exhibitions showed up in the outfield and under the stands. Real estate agents with relatives on city council had plans to demolish the place and put up something that would bring in more bucks. Most of its life the building has been living under threat. Even in the past few years there have been people with ice trays for hearts smiling while they dream of bulldozers off Ontario Street. These are the folks who wanted, also in 1971, to replace Christ Church Cathedral at Burrard and Georgia with a square glass office tower.

The last I heard, now that two baseball fans have bought the team, the Nat seems to be safe, though hemmed in a little. The bulldozer people are turning their attention to the demolition of, oh, the CBC, and well, the city's museum.

Kosmik Leagues and art galleries (and now a farmer's market every Saturday in the parking lot on the Ontario side) could never faze the joint. When the Vancouver Mounties were the tenants, you never knew what to expect. The Mounties appeared one Sunday with red uniform jerseys, though they had enough restraint not to adopt RCMP hats. Purists were, as they so often are, alarmed. "They look like a softball team," exclaimed some. "This will never catch on in baseball," said others. "What next, white shoes?" scoffed one worthy. "Not after Labour Day," said his wife. "These guys don't play much after Labour Day," replied her husband.

One July day in 1962, pitcher George Bamberger, the most adored player in the history of Vancouver professional baseball, strolled out to the mound with a radio transmitter concealed in his jersey. Bamby was the smartest hurler in the Pacific Coast League. Did he need advice on how to pitch to

the Tacoma Giants? No, manager Jack McKeon just wanted
to see what would happen once the league poobahs found out
that the Vancouver manager was managing over the airwaves.
Sure enough, a rule was added to the PCL charter — no more
Dick Tracy stuff.

1962 was a great year at the the building. The Mounties
did finish seventh that year, but so what? The Hollywood
Stars had come out to play in shorts and tall socks in 1950, but
twelve years later Cap Stadium had visitors from outer space!
Late during a cold night in May, with about 600 shivering
fans in the Cap, a huge flying saucer swooped over the city
and performed a fiery fly-by of Little Mountain. Vancouver
Mounties and Portland Beavers raced off the field under the
eerie light. The grandstand emptied as fans held tight to their
anti-freeze bottles and ran for the trees. After the interplanet-
ary vehicle had departed for the skies of Idaho, a lot of the fans
and the majority of the ballplayers returned to the scene, not
including Bert Cueto, the Cuban pitcher who had been on
the mound for the home team when the aliens arrived. Bad
enough, thought Cueto, that you have play in arctic weather,
but when the between-innings promotions get out of hand,
I'm out of here.

A UFO in the PCL. You could look it up. There ought to
be a plaque in the concourse at the Nat.

If you come to the park when the season opens at last, you
might not get to see a flying saucer, but chances are that you
will see young athletes in red shirts. And if you look in the
right direction you might see one of those old coots I was
talking about. He's the ghost of my pal Bud Kerr, who was
called up a couple of years ago. Bud liked to call himself a
baseball historian. He could tell you who played third base
for the Northwest League Champion Vancouver Capilanos

in 1947. He has his name on a bunch of seats in the grandstand, and people say that he used to sleep at the park. But he went to every game, including all the University of British Columbia games played at the Nat in late winter. Bud was at the very first game played at Capilano Stadium. Heck, he was the only guy I know who was in the stands the last time the Chicago Cubs won the World Series.

If you see his ghost, ask him how cold it was the night the Martians flew over.

# A Blazing High Hard One
## (More on the Night of the UFO)

*A lot of goofy stuff has happened at Nat Bailey Sta-*
dium. When I was a young man I saw the Vancouver Mounties baseball team take the field in those red uniforms! Organized baseball laughed them out of town. Imagine — coloured
baseball outfits! Thank goodness that never caught on, eh?

You should have been there for the 1962 season. I recently
published a book of stories about Vancouver in 1962, and I
guess my favourite one took place at the ball park. As you
know, the Mounties would finish in seventh place in 1962, but
they gave us baseball fans a season full of laughs. In the second
game of a doubleheader on July 18, manager Jack McKeon,
remember, stuck a radio receiver inside the jersey of his ace
pitcher George Bamberger. It wasn't that Jack was going to
tell Bamberger what to throw. Bamby was the most famous
pitcher in the Pacific Coast League, and knew more than anyone in the world what to throw at the starting lineup of the
Tacoma Giants. The manager just wanted to see whether he
could get away with it.

You could look it up. The radio kit was approved by the
Canadian government, and had the call letters XM11495.
Vancouver won the game 8-4, but the radio was not the rea-

son. During the course of the athletic endeavour, the first baseman got hit in the chest by a pickoff attempt he didn't know was coming. Jack should have given him a radio.

They had to make a few adjustments. In the first inning Bamberger called time and huddled with McKeon.

"Skipper," he said. "I can't hear you. I'm getting this disk jockey Red Robinson. He just played a song called 'Vacation' by some girl named Connie somebody. It's a real stinker of a song, Skip."

Organized baseball stepped in. They didn't like radio transmitters any more than they liked red uniforms.

There are a few things that organized baseball can't do anything about — like fans from outer space. They came on the night of May 28, 1962, and you could look it up in the May 29 Vancouver *Province* or the *Flying Saucer Review*, for all I know. The Mounties and the Portland Beavers, two squads with .240 team batting averages, got through nine innings without getting a runner past second base. Portland's Dante Figueroa had given up four hits, and the home team's Dagoberto Cueto, one of five Cubans on the roster, had given up six.

Both teams got through the tenth without incident, and there must have been a lot of real fans in attendance, because it can get cool in late May around 10 p.m., but most of the 660 witnesses were still in their seats. Forty-three of them were in possession of small containers of alcohol derived from grain. Señor Cueto walked the first two Beavers in the top of the eleventh. It was 41°F, about 40 degrees below the temperature in Havana. It was 10:40. From then until 10:45, according to the Vancouver *Sun*, Capilano Stadium was lit up by an unearthly light.

Here are some of the things the frightful object was called:

"a flaming airliner," "a burning satellite," "an off-course rocket," "a comet," and "a flying saucer."

The ballplayers took to their heels, and the 610 folks in the stands ran for the exits. All over the city automobiles were banging into each other as drivers stuck their heads out windows. Around Boise, Idaho five minutes later, people raised shotguns and rifles and opened up on the monstrous thing.

But a baseball game is not over 'til the last man is out. After a half hour of big eyes and agitated footsteps the umpires waved the Vancouver fielders and the Portland baserunners back onto the field. A Beaver named Ron Debus stepped into the batter's box. Everyone was set to go — two on, none out, top of the eleventh. But there wasn't any pitcher. Jack McKeon sent his batboy and his second-string catcher to look everywhere for Bert Cueto. The six-foot four-inch 170-pound righthander from San Luis was nowhere to be found. Either he had been abducted by the UFO or he had had a bad reaction to flaming saucers. His civilian pants and shirt were hanging on a peg in the Mounties' dressing room.

You want to know the final score? Now *there*'s a baseball fan!

# Some Tips on Becoming a Successful Loudmouth Baseball Fan

DON'T: When you are heckling the umpire, try to avoid obvious jokes about sightlessness. Really subtle cracks are all right. You could, for example, holler, "Sounded like a strike to me, Ump!"

DO: Shout variations of famous baseball sayings. This way you can show your knowledge of the game while impressing the people in your section with your wit. If the opposing team makes two errors, you might want to yell, "Hit 'em where they are!"

DON'T: If the visitors get a sacrifice fly in the top of the ninth to go ahead by a run, do not cheer because our outfielder caught the ball. I have seen this happen at Nat Bailey, and I had to wonder: who *are* these people?

DO: Sing loudly at the seventh-inning stretch. Sing, "Take me out to the ball game," even if you are already at the ball game. When the second line comes around, sing, "Take me out with the crowd." It is not "to" the crowd. Sheesh!

DON'T: Don't rip the home team. Be encouraging. If the opposition has the bases loaded with nobody out, I like to shout, "Now you got 'em where they want you!" If the opposition gets four extra-base hits in a row, I bellow, "That's it, keep mowin' them down!"

DO: Dress right. If you're wearing a baseball cap, wear the peak forward. You don't have to worry about sun on the back of your neck in Vancouver. Do not wear New York Yankee clothes, unless you are a tourist shopping on Robson Street, and then get something in pink. If you are in your team uniform, let's see your socks.

DON'T: I might get into trouble with management on this one. Don't yell, "Go, Cees, Go!" You are not at a hockey game. You have to be creative and witty when it comes to cheering at a baseball game. On the other hand, my friend Paul yells, "Go, Habs, Go!" at the Vancouver Canadians' games. Now, *that*'s witty.

DO: Try to think of something hilarious to yell at visiting ballplayers with interesting names. When "Poochy" Delgado came to town a few years ago, my friends in section 9 would bark every time he came to the plate. Try not to be obscene unless it is really funny and the kids won't understand.

DON'T: Don't boo the visitors' pitcher for throwing to first. He is trying to keep the runner from getting a jump. That is called baseball. Don't cheer just because one of our batters hits the ball high to the outfield. A fly ball is bad strategy unless it results in a sacrifice fly. You can cheer a sacrifice fly if it is performed by our team in a tight game.

DO: Go ahead and yell, "We want a hit!" But once in a while change your pitch. For example, you can yell, "We want world peace!" One I particularly like is "We want an early election!"

Okay, you are ready. Finish that hotdog, and give your lungs a workout.

— GEORGE BOWERING
*Official loudmouth fan
of the Vancouver Canadians*

# Two Bits on the Green Guy

*Is my team ploughing?*

— A.E. HOUSMAN

*In the year 2010 my wife Jean and I attended four* season's home openers with George Stanley — in Seattle, Victoria, Maui and Vancouver. He is the author of a terrific book of poems called *Opening Day*, a title any self-respecting baseball fan poet would wish to have thought of first. But George Stanley's on first. In case you wanted to know.

Well, he is in *Richard III*, Act v, Scene 3, but that's in another field.

George Stanley and I have been going to baseball games together since Connie Mack put away his catcher's mitt. I thought I might tell you ten of the things we do at the ball game.

## 1. *The anthems*

George likes to get there in time to hear the national anthems. I don't, so I usually loiter in the concourse while they are being sung with far too many syllables by some young female pop star wannabe. But George stands up and takes off his hat (though he doesn't do that silly USAmerican bit about trying to locate a cap bearing an ad for a transmission company over one's heart). I keep my cap on 'til the USAmerican song about weapons and so on is over. When the Canadian anthem starts, George sings good and loud, making sure we hear him intone "in all of us command." I don't sing at all, because the song is racist, sexist, religionist and anti-grammatical. In Maui a guy sang the Mexican national anthem because the visiting team was the Tijuana Cimarrones. He sang the chorus and all ten stanzas.

## 2. *His brother Gerald*

Gerald is the guy who knows everything about games and has a dry sense of humour. Not just baseball. Gerald can tell you the name of the Pittsburgh Steelers' backup quarterback. It is twice as much fun when Gerald comes to a ball game with us. A few years ago in Seattle, when George was 66 and I was 64 and Gerald was 63, Gerald picked up tickets for us — at the seniors' price. When we reported this to my daughter, chuckling with naughtiness, she said, "Oh you pulled a fast one on them!"

## 3. *The eighth inning*

George hates the eighth inning. He thinks they should jump straight from the seventh inning to the ninth inning. He hates the bottom of the eighth a little less, but he really detests the top of the eighth. He has a haunted look around his eyes in the break after the bottom of the seventh. If the visiting team loads the bases in the top of the eighth but doesn't score a run, he is a wet dishrag 'til the end of the game.

### 4. *Those little doughnuts*

George will ignore those little doughnuts, even if the fragrance made by their preparation pervades section 5 of the grandstand. But when Augie comes from Toronto for his annual vacation, wearing his old Vancouver Canadians AAA Champions tee-shirt, or when Andy's grandson Tyber comes down from Terrace in July, George springs for those little doughnuts. Sometimes I get one, even though Jean is there.

### 5. *The old guys wave*

When some attendees at Nat Bailey Stadium start the wave, thus proving that we are in 1970 and a hick town, George Stanley and I do not rise or throw our hands into the air. We sit there and let the wave pass over us. Sometimes I get up and raise my hands after the wave has passed two sections to our left or right. But we do do the old guys wave. George gets up very slowly, shakily, looking as if he will not be able to achieve the standing position, then agonizingly raises his skinny old arms a little bit higher than his head. Then like an aching tortoise he reacquires a sitting position, sometimes falling into it at last. Then I count to three and begin my own laborious ascent from my seat beside him. In the time we consume accomplishing this feat a normal ballpark wave could have washed over us eight times.

## 6. *The seventh inning stretch*

As soon as the third out of the top half of the seventh inning has been recorded, George gets to his feet, and I follow almost immediately. For a while we are the only spectators standing. Then the voice on the PA system tells the crowd that it is time for the seventh inning stretch, at which point most of the people in the stands begin to get it. We sing the cherished old song enthusiastically. I make sure that I shout the WITH of "take me out WITH the crowd," because 99 percent of the rubes around us intone, "to the crowd." When it comes to "one, two, three strikes yer out," I always make a point of getting stuck after "two." George likes that. Then, if the home team loses the game, George says, "It's a shame."

## 7. *Shouting stuff*

There are things we shout at every game, such as, "Rodriguez? What kind of baseball name is that?" Or when another visiting player is announced: "Never heard of him!" When an opposing pitcher lets loose an errant fastball: "Craaaazy wild!" George has a specific rule about this. He says that you can holler anything you want at a ball game. It can be any part of speech. "Nevertheless!" he once bellowed. That was a poet speaking.

## 8. *The chicken dance*

If the entertainment organizers cause the song "YMCA" to be played on the PA between innings, George and I do the actions, but I always forget how to do the bodily spelling.

George always gets it right, and I grumble about how difficult baseball can be. But I am getting so that I remember the sequence for the chicken dance. George, though, is again the master. His fingers, wings, hips, clap-clap are just simply superior. Next to the Vancouver Canadians co-owner Jeff Mooney, George Stanley is the best dancer in the yard.

## 9. *The sushi race*

Some years back the Milwaukee Brewers baseball people decided to hold a sausage race, every home game featuring a race from right field around to first base by three, then four people dressed as giant sausages — bratwurst, Italian, etc. Then the Washington Nationals had a race among four people dressed as giant Mount Rushmore heads — Lincoln, Jefferson, etc. Pretty soon more and more ballparks had such races. There are now racing perogies in Pittsburgh, for example. At Nat Bailey, we have the sushi race, a run on the infield warning track from first base around to third base, between a huge round Ms. BC Roll, Mr. Kappa Maki, and Chef Wasabi. The tradition is that Chef Wasabi, with his martial arts headscarf, never wins, often suffering a loss of attention. But when Jean Baird and George Stanley and I get out our quarters to bet on the race, George always bets his 25 cents on the big green blob. He maintains that the law of averages is on his side.

## 10. *The third inning rule*

George Stanley says that going for a hotdog or a beer before the third inning is just not done. He sneers at the long lineup that forms at the beer counter even before the national anthems. The moment that the ball goes plop into some visiting player's glove to signify the end of the second inning, George is on his feet, hand in his money pocket. "George," I object. "Is it really the third inning if the Vancouver pitcher has not released his first pitch in the direction of the plate?" "Mere casuistry," he replies, and off he goes to get his hotdog. Never a hamburger. Never a bratwurst or a foot-long or a smokie. Always the ordinary hotdog. He proclaims it good. I tried one once. Boy!

Poets belong at the ballpark, is what I am endeavoring to illustrate. George Stanley, author of *The Stick*, is living proof. In his Portland Beavers tee-shirt and cap, he represents the vital connection between a polis and its custodians of the divine art.

*Artie Gold as Light Fixture*

*Jack Spicer always said that he didn't care if his poems* weren't being read in New York or Duluth; he had an audience in the Bay Area for the 250 copies someone might print. In the middle of 1965 he died at age 39, and that was that for a while. When I arrived as a writer in residence in Montréal in 1967 I didn't expect to find anyone who had read Jack Spicer. But nothing could have prepared me for the young man who went by the signature "A. Gold." Not only had he read Spicer, but he wanted to *be* Spicer, as long as he could also be Frank O'Hara, another poet not habitually read by the literary and academic folks on that island in the St. Lawrence River.

It was not until 1975 that the San Francisco poet was published to a wider geography, in that year's *Collected Books of Jack Spicer*. Spicer's practice was not to write occasional poems or loose lyrics, but to be working on a book, and he had a lot of personal procedural rules about what that entailed. Sometimes Artie worked on a book. But if you saw his kitchen or his shoulder bag you would see great heaps of paper upon which A. Gold poems were handwritten or typed. People would see him coming and duck back into the alley, unwilling to spend their whole weekend reading these newest pages.

Still, I think that it is a good idea to gather the books of Artie Gold into one volume. And there are rumors that some of the other hundreds of poems that have not totally disappeared will constitute another volume some time somewhere, just as a collected Spicer has now been published.

I make the Spicer connection partly because of Artie's avowed interest, of course, and partly because I know how the official literature custodians can and do ignore the most interesting poetry being written in their country. Since 1967 I have seen a lot of good young poets arrive, and I have been so damned glad that they can still find their way somehow to my ears. When Artie died at age 60 who could believe he was ever that age? He passed on Valentine's Day 2007, the most garrulous poet who ever had to hide away from people because of his allergies. And the obits writer from a Montréal daily asked me whether he should spend space on this "poet," or was he "just another of those Montréalers revered for their admirably careless lifestyles?"

Artie used to send you surprises in the mail, strange objects, drawings he made of you years ago, little geodes, words that had to be dangled in the window's light before you could make them out. His poems could be like that, too. He had an acutely sensitive ear and a willingness to make sounds you would never expect. His images leaped from porch rail to nose cone, and he wove smart-alec irony through sharp threads of emotion. You knew that he was watching, and that his amused eyes were on you when you lifted your face from the page.

Life handed Artie a lot of miserable obstacles from the beginning, some old family sadness you would never hear all of, bad lungs that could not abide the cats he liked so much, hunger for company he had to avoid more and more. Maybe he really was a *poète maudit*, as he is often limned; but I don't remember elsewhere seeing such a combination of gift and application in a young practitioner. And just now I caught a glimpse of the look on his face that told me how funny he thinks that sentence is.

In my introduction to *cityflowers* you will find my delight in the sheer capability of this Montréal poet in his twenties, so much unlike the others with their academic structures and desire to express themselves. All these years later I still don't know how that young man found the means to educate himself so well. As I have said, his only contemporary in 1969 Montréal was Dwight Gardiner, who also loved Spicer and O'Hara. By 1974, Gardiner was in Vancouver, working at Talonbooks, where he designed *Even yr photograph looks afraid of me*.

I was living in Vancouver too, and for a while Artie came out to live here, where he would teach west coast poets to guard their refrigerators and practice their irony. Artie had previously spent time in California, but the Pacific was really no place for A. Gold — he needed to be within reach of the chicken liver at Snowden Deli.

Little Gold books came out just about every year in the seventies, and in their unique bindings and designs they illustrated Artie's penchant for curios. *Mixed Doubles*, co-authored with Geoff Young and hand-printed at The Figures in San Francisco, looks like a tennis court, complete with net. *5 Jockeypoems* comes as a fold-out inside an envelope, produced by a sympatico Montréal bookstore, The Word. *Some of the cat poems* is a handy chapbook that also features Artie's witty and precise cat drawings, as well as a preface by "The shortstop of the heart." Though I was a shortstop at the time, the preface is not by me this time, but by Artie himself, his catself. *before Romantic Words* came out at the end of the decade, and in my copy Artie wrote "many years in the preparation." a description that, if you read through the poems, seems patently untrue, unless by this time Artie was Jack Spicer and Frank O'Hara.

My introduction to Artie's selected *The Beautiful Chemical Waltz* contains remarks about poems that were in the books mentioned above. It could almost serve as an introduction to the present collection, and I stand by everything I wrote there. I did not see my young friend very often in the last years of his life — once when he was dumpster-diving for antiques in some happening part of downtown Montréal, finally at the door of his apartment on west Sherbrooke. I went to Montréal to attend his memorial at The Word bookstore on April 14, 2007, where I was pleased to find that the place was jammed and the chicken livers were delicious. All the people Artie had to stay away from were crowded in, an allergic's nightmare. I met Artie's brother for the first time. The poets he had worked with at Véhicule were there, all grown adults. I felt like a ghost, and thought about wafting through Artie's world. I found myself inside my favourite A. Gold poem, "R. W. 11." I used to tell young poets to stay away from similes, and now I was brought to my knees by the figure that ends that poem.

*Originally published as the Introduction to* THE COLLECTED BOOKS OF ARTIE GOLD.

# Pages I Have Trouble With 1:
## Quicksand on the Dining Room Floor

*I was reading a novel called* THE RAIN ASCENDS *by* Joy Kogawa, a book published in 1995, some time after her novel *Itsuka* and the various versions of the popular *Obasan*.

According to the quotations printed on the cover and half-title page of the paperback I was reading, major Canadian reviewers liked *The Rain Ascends*, saying that it "wrestles beauty out of torment," that the language provides "beauty and integrity," and that it is "like a globe of spun crystal." The author is said to be quiet and compassionate, and over and over, beauty is proclaimed.

I think that the reviewers were thinking that what they had found here is "poetic" storytelling. Maybe the author did, too. But I soon ran into trouble, trying to open myself to the persuasion of poetry, as one does, and not just charitably.

Chapter 2 threw me into a tizzy. It presents a person referred to as "you" going downstairs to see her aged father sitting in front of a fireplace. This could have been handled nicely, offering some images for one's receptive eyes. I like a novel or story that offers images I can see, and so I drop my defences and look. This works well with Ernest Hemingway and Margaret Atwood.

All right. Here "you" is seen first at the top of the creaky stairs, "in the long moment before diving." But then, no, we realize she is not bent on personal injury, but rather takes the stairs slowly. As she tentatively descends one stair at a time we see "pages torn from the heart's walls and flung onto the debris-covered floor." So we see that whoever is down there is untidy, and we take that as characterization, but there are too many of those blood-smeared pages for us to see anything clearly.

Then all at once "you" is as if at the racetrack, like "a race horse at the starting line, pawing the track." I try to erase all thought of a starting gate and see, perhaps a less formal competition. And, yes, I think I have heard people say that horses "paw" at the ground, though that seems the wrong kind of foot. Then "you" hears the "starting gun" with a "sharp retort like a dull roar." Sharp and dull are usually taken to be opposites, so the author here is likely employing contradiction for metaphorical purposes; but I wouldn't have thought such a one useful, because starter's pistols do not usually roar.

In any case, "you" descends to this messy, noisy place while holding the bannister "with both hands." Despite that, we see "your dangerous weapon of half-truths clutched tight in your shaking hand." That's where I gave up counting hands. But then, shock on shock, the weapon becomes an operating room "instrument," and "you must make the incision as precisely as a surgeon." In case the reader thinks that this will just be another case of pages ripped off a heart, "you have donned your mask, your gloves." Then we learn that "what is required is to see the face behind the face, the hideous face of Mr. Hyde that you know is there, but that you have not once, not ever, seen."

For a while this reader was uncertain whether it was "you's" own face or that of another that is here referred to, and entertained the notion that this ambiguity must be a strength of the fiction so far. Furthermore, having been alerted by the copy on the cover of the book that this novel is about a daughter and her aged father, we are compelled to remind ourselves that in Stevenson's narrative Mr. Hyde is described as a young man and quite small.

In any case, in the next paragraph we are told that "you" now sees a dining room fireplace with flames in it, with a man sitting in front of it, and she approaches him with fear and love. Soon we are told that this is "you's" father, and that he was a god, creator of the land, and that now he is old, in a house to which the mist clings. We are then provided with a great number of adjectives attached to him, sometimes four or five to the sentence. Again we find contradiction — right after we see his "body shrunken with age," he is "larger than life." This commonplace figure of speech is followed by others as we are told that he is a contradictory personage.

Yes, there are a lot of adjectives, so many that one starts to ward them off. There is a lot of figurative language where concrete imagery would have made for guilelessly persuasive narrative. Some of the metaphors are clichés or just bad choices: "I do not know how he survives the quicksand of his own paradoxical being." Quicksands of being are best left to the highschool novelist. Quicksand does not go well with a floor littered with stuff, anyway.

Kogawa, when she trusts the language, can be much better than that, as she was most of the time in *Obasan*. Here in Chapter 2 of this book, she can give us an image rather than a creaking nightmare of the father figure: "He is crouched slightly forward on the leather elephant stool, his now stooped and fragile frame wrapped in the old wine velour bathrobe

Mother gave him many Christmases ago. His face is roughly shaven, the long white brows untrimmed." One might have removed one adjective, but that is otherwise clear writing, something to reach toward.

Ah, but then, this: "Years and years ago when you first learned about the deep fissure in his life, you plastered it over with mud and wordlessness. But Eleanor's midnight storms have washed away the patchwork and the crack in the foundation of your heart lies deeply exposed." Mud and wordlessness? Now, the crack in "you's" heart that replaces the one in the father's life is again probably usefully confused. But please, no more mud — it is messy enough in here already.

"You" says for a second time (though the narrator forgets, and says that "you" is repeating it a third time) that she could not sleep. The father does not reply, and as she was going to dive earlier, now "you can feel the pressure, a visceral force [do we require both?] within you [where viscerae properly are] as you prepare to leap." But once again, "you" does not leap, and in a shower of adjectives and adverbs, the old man makes his shuffling pathetic departure. After he has gone, "you" looks into the fireplace and sees that he has been burning letters. We observe "one red ribbon curled like a comma," which the text goes on to explain is a "half-burnt punctuation mark." It is meant, we are pretty sure, to be a symbol.

I was left at the end of this short chapter, hoping that the rest of the book would be less poeticized, and fondly remembering the clear economical descriptions of the scenes in *The Strange Case of Dr. Jekyll and Mr. Hyde*.

*Poetry Summer*

*In 1960, Grove Press published an anthology that* would help to split USAmerican poetry into two. Three years earlier Donald Hall had published an anthology titled *New Poets of England and America*, with an introduction by Robert Frost. The USAmerican poets included were from the conventional, academic side of the playground, what Ron Silliman would come to call the poetry of quietude. There one could read samples from people such as Donald Justice, Robert Lowell and May Swenson. Three years later, Donald M. Allen's *The New American Poetry* would include none of the poets in the Hall anthology. The Beats and the San Francisco poets, the Black Mountain guys and the New York "school" would be to USA poetry what bebop had been to USA music, or what the action painters had been to USA art, what Marlon Brando and James Dean were to USA moviemaking.

In 1963, hardly any professors in the USA or Canada had heard of the poets in the Allen anthology. But Warren Tallman at the University of British Columbia had, and over the past few years he and his wife Ellen had arranged visits to Vancouver by some of them. Frail but flamboyant, Tallman got the help of others and put together a summer school pro-

gram at UBC, three weeks of credit courses to be conducted
by instructors Charles Olson, Robert Creeley, Robert Duncan, Denise Levertov, Allen Ginsberg and Margaret Avison.
Avison left early due to health problems in her family, but the
other five, in the same spot for the first time in their lives,
taught seminars at UBC, conducted impromptu classes and
gave public readings both at the university and all over town.

For my companions and me, this was an amazing opportunity to hang out with our heroes and meet their other followers
from around the continent. We wrote seminar notes, and kept
journals about those unprecedented three weeks. Some of
these jottings and writings were excerpted in *Olson: The Journal of the Charles Olson Archives*, Number 4, Fall 1975. In addition to a transcription of a joint session of the "instructors,"
there are notes by Clark Coolidge, Pauline Butling, Daphne
Marlatt, and me.

In addition to this journal, the poems I was writing at the
time, and letters to writers in other cities, I wrote some bits in
the simple diary I had been keeping since 1958. On looking
back at the diary, I am struck by the naïveté of this young aco-
lyte, and cannot believe that my friends were that innocent
and awkward.

*Thursday, July 25, 1963. 12:32 a.m.*

A curious man, this Allen Ginsberg. I mean after all the
fable, the very good & purifying thing to see him wandering
around Warren Tallman's back yard. Hearing his voice in a
classroom, ruminating & NY slurring of afterthoughts as on
the recordings. I was struck early with how handsome he is;
this despite, maybe, his bald top and long ringlets, & fine full
curly Jewish Hebrew Joshua beard like I used to see in the
color plates of my old bible. And of course despite his absolute

humanism I am shy of him, as I always am of my elders and betters, tho I hide behind the security of letters.

### Monday, July 29, 1963. 5:45 p.m.

Wow. Right now, while we are looking for a place for her, Carol Bergé and her son Peter, are staying here at our house. Also Phil Whalen showed up, and I got a chance to talk w/ him this aft, also talking to Ginsberg. Other people here met whose names I'd seen someway, John Keys, A. Fredric Franklyn. And I'm trying to tutor twice a day! Today Lionel introduced me to Charles Olson. Big man reaching down to shake my hand. Impossible to register, sitting w/ Carol Bergé, Lionel Kearns and David Bromige, watching up front of room — Duncan, Creeley, Ginsberg, Olson, Whalen, talking it out, and meeting questions from the floor.

### Tuesday, July 30, 1963. 10.54 p.m.

Last night Phil Whalen did the night session with a surprise reading, and he didn't come over very well — in fact Creeley, unshaven as all the poets, fell asleep in the middle & most of the way thru. Anyway, everybody could feel bad vibrations, and Whalen remarkt on them after his reading. And then there were some hostile questions from unknowing people in the audience, and after a while they swung favorable to him, & wound up asking for another poem, which he gave them, & then it was over. He seemed to get in the way of his reading, doing it diffidently, drinking water in middle of poem, says he'd rather be read.

### Thursday, August 1, 1963. 12:34 a.m.

Last night in July Allen Ginsberg read his poems in sequence, sometimes beautifully stepping back from the headlong passion, other times, as in "Sunflower Sutra," flying with oldtime exciting crack voice. This the first time I have heard him read in person, and wonderful thing is that after all the identity-personality fixation, he here in flesh, is first of all a person, and a rather handsomely, earnestly beautiful one — a quiet man who can honestly make loud noises. And in seminar the other day he spoke good truth to me about getting more greatly concerned with finding my personal reactions rather than finding form as a concern. And this helps the great new stage I'm recognizing in my poetry.

*Sunday, August 4, 1963, 8:34 p.m.*

### POET WHO WASN'T THERE
### GIVES REAL BEAT READINGS
by Mike Grenby

The bearded poet said he wasn't there, but the 350 people who paid $1.25 to come and see him Friday night certainly were.

They sat and stood crammed into a 250-seat classroom at the University of B.C. for an hour and a half, listening to a disjointed harangue laced with obscenity.

Allen Ginsberg, considered by some a leader of the beat generation, was reading his poetry.

In a recent interview with *The Sun* he said his body was walking around but he had disappeared.

But on Friday night he was sufficiently in his body to expound on beautiful boys, moving trees and hairy souls.

The frequently repeated obscenities brought embarrassed snickers and the occasional horse laugh from the sweltering audience of students, bearded poets, girls in shorts and adults in evening dress.

When Ginsberg paused in his reading, scattered applause broke out. Sometimes it didn't.

When in the middle of a poem, Ginsberg asked, "Is this interesting or not?" a few clapped and several people walked out.

After it was over, comments ranged from "interesting" to a repetition of one of Ginsberg's lines, "Oh I must be mad!"

This is the sort of bullshit that convinces me that I'm glad after all that I didn't go seriously into journalism. Though I know by now that this sort of business gets into poetry, too. This the most disappointing thing.

*Monday, August 5, 1963, 3:53 p.m.*

Today for the first time I went to Olson's seminar, and I got one specific (and there seems to be a dearth of them). The reason he goes to the root of a word becomes clear when you know that root is not a historical (fake) thing from which the word evolved; but rather the ROOT that is still there, feeding the branches we eat. That is, in 2100 AD we speak the same organic language(s) we spoke in 2100 BC, and there is no reason to fix that false historical date on it. God! it nirks to realize just how much has been put on us by that stepladder notion of history. And in sublime rural knowledge and wisdom, Olson knows.

*Wednesday, August 7, 1963, 8:18 p.m.*

Today I went to Creeley's class in the afternoon. (Red Lane, who arrived in town the same day my parents did — 5th — went to Ginsberg's seminar.) I took my new unlined notebook (actually a sketchbk) and made some notes, from wch something may eventually emerge.

I think, with these new publications, that it is time to narrow down the magazines in which I appear, slicing some of the catch-alls as I turn up in more favorable ones. I am torn, tho, between one of me that says any kind of restriction is lethal, and the other that says a man is known by the company he keeps. I know I wd rather be in *Evergreen* than in *Hudson*.

*Saturday, August 10, 1963, 8:52 p.m.*

Today, over at Robt Duncan's again, taping the poems that Frank and I wrote together for *Tish* in the winter of 1961–2; and wch Duncan has always shown interest in. And then Frank spoke of his interest in printing a pamphlet of them, in a small edition, and maybe done by the Rattlesnake Press of Oliver. I think it wdnt be a bad idea, if it didn't cost too much.

One of the first things to think of in Calgary, is to try to get backing for the mag I have in mind. The backing, tho, should not commit me to publishing Calgary and/or Can. poetry. I'll name it *Issue*, and it will have an issue to make each time, and feature one of my favorite poets, like *Origin*.

*Sunday, August 11, 1963, 9:06 p.m.*

Strange couple of nights last two, with Friday night a rambunctious party & orgy at the Wahs', where Duncan was holding de Sade session on the double bed, and Ginsberg was dashing around, kissing everyone. Angela was frightened at first, then joined in the orgy, with awed feeling. I sat and talkt with Denise Levertov for awhile, and she sd I was the only Vancouver poet she'd formed an image of, but that I was different. Then I sat in livingroom & watcht most of the night. Last night was very pleasant, starting in the Graduate Centre, and continuing at Warren's, where I spoke with Philip Whalen, & Angela spoke with Allen Ginsberg.

*Monday, August 12, 1963, 11:39 p.m.*

Tonight Creeley read poems and Chapter 17 of his novel, and had to read to candle light because of electrical storm, wch was nice, and good effect. Once more, while he was reading his novel I was struck by how similarly we have regarded things, & our own psychology reactions. There was one scene where he was "ineptly" making love to a girl on a hill, when a man interrupted to tell him to take her home, and he wanted to go back in time to tell the man to fuck off, but knew he cdnt, wasnt permitted to even if he cd go back, knew this years later, and I knew how he felt. I wish he knew that.

*Robin Blaser at the Griffins*

*For four decades Robin Blaser was one of the most* influential poets in the North American world, but he was not a household name. I presume that in your household the name Atwood has been mentioned, maybe the name Ginsberg. Most professors of Canadian literature still do not teach Blaser's work and probably have not read it either.

Yet he was a member of the Order of Canada. He collaborated with the British composer Harrison Birtwistle on the opera *The Last Supper*, which was commissioned by the Staatsoper of Berlin in 2000. His book of collected poems, *The Holy Forest*, was edited by Stan Persky and Michael Ondaatje, introduced by Robert Creeley, and published by Coach House Press in 1993. It is 400 pages long, and it is not light reading. The University of California Press edition of 2006 came in at 520 pages. On the dust jacket there is a photo of the author with his arms raised high. Next to him stands Scott Griffin, the famous benefactor of Canadian and other poetries.

Because on the night of May 31, 2006, at Toronto's Mac-Millan Theatre, Blaser was presented with the Life Time Recognition Award given by the trustees of the Griffin Trust for Excellence in Poetry.

Since 2000, the Griffin Trust has rewarded excellence in poetry written in English anywhere in the world, including translation of other poetries. Every spring there are two awards, one to a Canadian poet, and one to a poet from elsewhere. The night before the awards there is always a group reading by the seven poets on the shortlists.

Blaser was presented with his award after the intermission at that night's reading. USAmerican poet and Griffin Trustee Robert Hass made the presentation. Other trustees are writers Margaret Atwood, Carolyn Forché, Scott Griffin, Michael Ondaatje, Robin Robertson and David Young.

Blaser, a Vancouver resident since 1966, was born in Denver, Colorado, and brought up in numerous Idaho villages that no one has heard of, most of which have disappeared. But he was no desert hick — he studied piano, theatre, French and Latin, and even began to prepare for a life in the priesthood. Friends told him that all these things are obvious in his recondite poetry.

After a summer session at Northwestern University in Illinois, and a year at the College of Idaho at Caldwell, he departed in 1944 for the University of California in Berkeley. On his first day in town he attended a production of Euripides's *The Trojan Women*. Before long he was part of a poetry circle that included Robert Duncan and Jack Spicer. The three would form the nucleus of what would come to be called "the Berkeley Renaissance," and they would be in the centre of the hubbub that was San Francisco poetry in the late fifties and early sixties.

With master's degrees in arts and library sciences, Blaser took a job as a librarian at Harvard University, and then returned to the west coast to take a position at San Francisco State. In 1966, he was offered a professorship at Simon Fraser

University in Burnaby, BC, and was a distinguished and sought-after teacher there for twenty years. His classes were crowded with visitors from outside the SFU community. In 1986 he took early retirement and transformed himself into a university, becoming a learning resource for many poets who came to Vancouver to study with him. With Duncan and Spicer, Blaser developed what came to be known as the "serial poem," an extended form that is composed of sections related to one another without temporal or hierarchical order. They should be, in Spicer's word, "dictated verse," and they turned out to be scholarly.

Blaser's work is steeped in philosophical reference, yet remarkably lyrical. In an essay called "The Fire," he wrote "I want a nation in which discourse is active and scholarship is understood as it should be, the mode of our understanding and the ground of our derivations."

Early in his adult life Blaser fell under the spell of Dante, hence the title of his collected poems, the story of a scholar-poet wandering in the holy forest, where no authoritarian consciousness can declare meaning. His poems explore the world in multiple voices and views. So his poems are, while musical, also fragmentary, multidirectional, filled with quotations and allusions, resonant with the voices of philosophers and poets ancient and contemporary and often obscure.

But his purpose is not airy. The poems respond to the political events of our times, and Blaser often employed the term "public world," making homage to Hannah Arendt and Alfred North Whitehead. For Blaser, the challenge was always to combine the lyrical, which is usually associated with the first-person poem, with the public world. Thus the multiple voices, even in his songs.

In his last years Blaser further explored the relationship of poetry and music, not only with the aforementioned opera but also with choral music, such as a 2005 cycle of twelve songs for three singers created with composer David McIntyre. In these songs a soprano, a mezzo and a tenor wrap their voices around short poems spoken by what only appears to be a first person narrator.

Even in his eighties, the snowy-haired mentor-poet continued to travel and compose. The University of California Press published a volume of his collected essays to stand beside his collected poems.

The 2006 Lifetime Recognition Award from the Griffin Trust for Excellence in Poetry was richly deserved and an important acknowledgement of a great Canadian poet. And it was encouraging, the news that while this great scholar poet was largely ignored in his country's academies, his spirit and his language were properly attended to by its poets.

In 2008 Blaser would be back at the Griffin celebrations, to pick up the prize for best Canadian book of poetry.

There is an irony in the presumption that the universe contains the "collected" poems of Robin Blaser. Within the five hundred pages of *The Holy Forest* moves a lifetime's thought such as we are not used to or prepared for. Whitman was not fooling when he said that a poet, an extraordinary poet, can himself be a cosmos. But as sidereal as Blaser's lines become, we never forget that the purpose is our human living every day inside what is. Blaser was solemn enough to approach Dante Alighieri as a "Great Companion," and serious enough to maintain that "the truth is laughter."

Blaser was a great Canadian poet. Across the line, they still think of him as a great USAmerican poet, though he was with us up here for forty-five years. High in the mountains of Greece, the Gods think that he is their own gold medalist.

When the news spread that Robin Blaser had an inoperable brain tumour, people started flying to Vancouver to talk with him, one of the great privileges of our time. Blaser was a rare and recondite and luminous poet, and others loved him. Here is the right word: they *cherished* him. Now we have the poems, a treasure that arrived in our lifetime.

One is not at all embarrassed this time to speak in superlatives. When he wrote long poems addressed to Dante and Duncan as his great companions, we had no trouble going along with that. Robin Blaser did not put up with any crap from politicians or poets who would put themselves before the world and its languages. And he did everything with style. When one of us would push him in his wheelchair down to his chosen spot outside the hospital for a cigarette, he wore his favourite beret over the stitches in his skull. When we gathered at the hospice to be with his sleeping person in the last few days, we shared martinis and Blaser stories. Now I would like to suggest that once in a while we honour Robin by spending the early afternoon in our housecoats, reading Maimonides.

*On Reading Julian Rathbone's*
King Fisher Lives

*Jean and I went to Nuevo Vallarta for a week, and I* had thought that three books would get me through, but I finished them before we got to the airport for the trip home. So she gave me Julian Rathbone's novel *King Fisher Lives* for the plane. But she said that I could borrow it (though of course she herself had borrowed it from the library) only if I wrote a report on it.

What were the books I took with me, you ask. The first was *Don't Touch the Poet*, by Lyman Gilmore, a biography of the USAmerican poet Joel Oppenheimer, by a faculty member of the small college in New Hampshire to which Oppenheimer had escaped from a life below 14th Street in NYC. Gilmore's writing is hardly professional or scholarly, peppered with repetitions and errors as it is. He says, for example, that Margaret Randall left NYC and lived in New Mexico before going to Cuba. It was Mexico City, actually. Still, as a reader of writing by and about the poets of the Donald Allen anthology of 1960, I enjoyed discovering the details of Oppenheimer's life. I used to correspond with him back in the day.

The second book was *Strange Pilgrims*, a group of twelve short stories by Gabriel García Marquez. This is only the third book by the Colombian "magic realist" that I have read. I picked it up for 50 cents at the Vancouver Public Library toss-out sale. The stories are various in length, point-of-view, and a lot of other things, but held together, or so the author hoped, by the fact that each is about a character who has come at some time in the past from the Caribbean to a European place such as Barcelona or Paris. In translation, at least, the stories of García Marquez are highly readable, and you find yourself racing through them, they were so enjoyable. I should have brought a book by Michel Butor. When I finished the book I left it at the towel shack next to the pool, where some thick paperbacks by pop writers lay untouched. An hour later it was gone.

The third book was Gary Snyder's most recent book of talks and essays, *Back on the Fire*. Because many of the pieces in the collection were talks given to groups interested in ecology or Japan, there is quite a lot of repetition. For example, about eight times you find out that Snyder is now opposed to the forest service idea that all forest fires have to be fought against. In among the forest/mountain pieces you find stuff about other poets, such as Allen Ginsberg, Philip Whalen and Ko Un. I liked these bits the best.

Jean took six books down with her, I think. But she has to read a lot because she is assembling her famous report on the Booker Prize winners. I know, as I told you, why she loaned me the Rathbone book. She knows you have to bribe me to read a novel by an Englishman of the past half-century, unless it is John Berger or B.S. Johnson. But it was either Julian Rathbone or the Air Transat magazine for four and a half hours.

Rathbone is, apparently, the author of several exotic thrillers of the sort that the Brits have always liked — *Mr. Midshipman Easy* and all that — romances in which some Brit of either sex goes to Tangiers or Bangladesh to risk all instead of growing old in stodgy Blighty. There is a chassis of that model in this novel, but it looks in this case as if Rathbone wanted to write something that the university crowd would accept without a plain brown wrapper.

The title character is a American writer who comes to a Brit university as artist in residence, misbehaves in the sixties manner, produces a barenaked version of *Timon of Athens*, scoops up a local academic novelist's half-sister, and becomes a naked caveman in a secluded Spanish valley. Along the way, Rathbone makes sure that we get the parallels to Timon as well as *Lord of the Flies*, and we think also of *Heart of Darkness*. So we get homosexuality, incest, drugs, alcohol and cannibalism.

This is apparently Rathbone's regular fare, but here, as I said, he tries to dress it up with a kind of stock literary theory of the avant-garde, even spelling it out in the second-to-last section, where a Spanish professor in Unamuno country goes on about narrative and reality. One good feature of the book, and the likely reason for Jean's lending it to me, is the multiplicity of styles — we get questionable narratives from several sources, plus TV interview transcription, scholarly introductions, letters, journals, notes, lecture, etc.

So can we accept the two most obvious problems with Rathbone's offering, or do we leave the book on the airplane and pay the library fine?

First of all, he seems to know little about the academic world: one scholar signs her name as a professor at "Milton University, Indiana," while we know that she would supply the city; and she claims that her thesis is a comparison of twentieth-century life with twentieth-century fiction. Oh, please!

The other problem? Do you remember those British movies in which would appear an "American" character played by an English actor who only thinks that he has the accent right? The badly-behaved American writer Rathbone presents us with here seems to this reader to resemble nothing more than a middle-class self-involved Brit trying to appear wild. But the real kicker? That character refers to a two-week period as a "fortnight."

*Pages I Have Trouble With 2:*
*Indian Coastlines*

*When Rita Wong's* FORAGE, *published by Nightwood* Editions, won the Dorothy Livesay Poetry Prize in 2008, I thought that was all right. I can't remember which good books were ignored by the judging committee that year, but other than Wong's book, the shortlist was pretty punk, I recall. The whole business about book prizes has had a deleterious effect on writing and especially on publishing, but still, when you see a short list you do pick a book to cheer for, if only to avoid the rewarding of a real dog. It doesn't always work: remember the 1999 Giller Prize?

The cover of *Forage* is beautifully composed, and it depicts a fearful modern ugliness, a vast hill of discarded computer memory boards and other such refuse. The book takes on perhaps our most serious subject — the connections between political injustices and industrial destruction of the ecosphere. Here is most of the reason for my liking the book: it is interesting in formal design. Usually, and sadly, you can depend on the poet who takes on serious political and social issues to do so with literary forms that have been long approved by the bourgeoisie.

Really, the only thing I did not like about the form of the

work was the absence of upper-case letters and graphemic punctuation. These are the two "advances" that busloads of tyro poets hope will signify their modernity. Nowadays they look like nothing more than what you see on the screens of teenagers' cell phones. Talk about the conventional!

Wong works with the page as her unit here. Sometimes it will consist of a square of lower case prose. Sometimes the poem zips around the page like a puppy looking for a warm spot. Sometimes we seem to see what look like short lyrics. There are plenty of those postmodern parentheses beloved of graduate students in the English language: p a r e n t (h) e t (h) i c a l. There are a few photographs. And then there is the stuff written beside and sometimes beneath the poems. Some of this marginalia is done in Chinese written characters. Most of it appears to have been done in the author's handwriting (the Chinese written characters too?). Turning the book sideways, we may be reading notes about the writing of the poem, or more often quotations from Edward Sapir or Rachel Carson. There are also asterisks and footnotes.

All in all, the earnestness and skill of the work make the book, despite its targets, a pleasure to read. It is the poet's second volume, and does show a few signs of eager novelty-making. The only one that made me bite my teeth was this one: "she / tumults through school years." High school kids used to do that, I remember.

So what is the problem I want to bring attention to? Well, it lies more in an attribution than in a strophe by Ms Wong. What we might call the title poem, "forage, fumage," takes up two pages, has handwritten phrases down and up the margins, and is followed by three footnotes, the third being this: "It is not mere chance that the more inland provinces such as Quebec, Manitoba, Ontario, and Saskatchewan bear Indian names while the maritime provinces or external coastal zones such as Newfoundland, Prince Edward Island, Nova Scotia, New Brunswick, British Columbia and Northwest Territories carry names with European origins. The political economy of conquest and trade can give more detailed answers than philology." This is identified as a quotation from Marwan Hassan in a book titled *Velocities of Zero*.

If you Google about you will find quite a few academics named Marwan Hassan, but if you look for the title you will find that it is a book published in 2002 by TSAR Publications. That's the book-publishing branch of a journal called *The South Asian Review* — not the University of Pittsburgh magazine of that name, but a much more recent Toronto journal for Canadian immigrants from Asia who are interested in literature and identity politics. Mr Hassan is described by Google as a fiction writer. His books have been issued by an Ottawa publisher that I must admit was unknown to me. Its name is Common Redpoll Books, and information about it is hard to find, such as the names of other authors it publishes.

Well, to get back to "forage, fumage," the poem is about the Indian names for North American places (I am willing, for the sake of argument, to go along with Mr Hassan's name for the Natives of the Americas) and the non-Indian names that have replaced them. It starts a little wonkily, I think: "from the georgia strait to the florida strait, it sounds so americanned." I am going to assume that Ms Wong means that the canning was done not so much by Americans as by the USA. Yet, in a poem that purports to be sensitive to place names and their origin, we should expect to hear that BC's strait was named for a British king, and that Florida's bears a Spanish name. (Ms Wong, at the time of the book's writing, was dividing her time between Vancouver and Miami.) Anyway, the poem proceeds in an instructive and entertaining way, ending with the aforementioned quotation from Mr Hassan.

That's what I have trouble with. Let me start at the beginning. I do not believe that it is enough to say "it is not mere chance." I have found that when people say that, they are not well prepared to say what it is if it is not mere chance. Sometimes that phrase is used by conspiracy theorists. Does Mr Hassan suggest that a conspiracy was responsible for the naming of the Canadian provinces as they were? He does seem to suggest that if you happen to have a province on the edge of the ocean, chances are that it will have a European name. I would still like to have a better argument than that.

But let's have a look at those province names. Three of the provinces that are called "more inland" by Mr Hassan have shorelines on the ocean, these being Quebec, Ontario and Manitoba. On the other hand, Alberta, one of our two land-locked provinces, was named after a member of the British royal family, just as the Strait of Georgia was. That naming was not done by chance, I agree; it was done by her husband, who was the Governor-General of Canada.

Of course, wherever the European sailors and politicians went they named things after what they knew back home. It was a way of fending off the fear of the unknown. That's why, when they saw a bird that was a bit red up front they called it a "robin," though it did not otherwise resemble the English bird. For other examples, check out the "salmon" or "magpie." Look at early European paintings of the St Lawrence valley and notice the ancient European trees growing along the river's banks.

To get personal for a while, I might report that I grew up in the interior of British Columbia, mostly in the Okanagan Valley. When I was a boy that valley was full of fruit trees, by the way, though a few feet from the trees you would find sagebrush, cactuses and tumbleweeds. I grew up surrounded by Indian names, some of them attached to places, some of them to human beings, though the ones attached to human beings were often European. So I was born in Penticton, and spent a lot of my childhood in Osoyoos, Kaleden, Kelowna, Tonasket, Omak, Wenatchee and Keremeos.

Well, it is true that I was a boy in a "maritime province," but I was 400 road kilometers from the coast. Maybe that coastline was peppered with the colonists' christenings. But wait — when I moved to the coast I had to remember how to spell Coquitlam, Nanaimo, Qualicum, Tsawwassen and Squamish, not to mention Tacoma, Tillamook and Chehalis. I am betting that as a fellow growing up in British Columbia I knew a lot more Indian names than I would have growing up in Ontario, that "more inland" province.

You will notice that I am not calling down Rita Wong's book or even her poem. I am just reporting a snag in my reading, and paying attention to an idea I picked up long ago as a young poet trying to learn — that a poem is not a jewel to be appraised by a jeweler, as I was instructed by my New Critics-reading English 101 professor, but rather the field to be entered by readers who are interested in learning more by interlocution. There is so much curiosity and attention and brain in Rita Wong's *forage*, that you really do want to get in on the conversation and that way see where she will alight next.

*Communication, Social Responsibility,*
*Politics, and Religion*

*i*

*Of course, one enjoys the fantasy that a reader some-*
where in Saskatchewan is holding one's book open and shaking his head in wonderment and respect at the sheer brilliance
of the writing. And though it makes me all shy, I am pleased
when I am told by someone I don't know that he or she really
likes my short stories, let us say. But the only reader I have in
mind while working is yours truly. I am so busy trying to hear
the line or sentence, that all else fades into the near distance.

Here is where I really admire Erin Mouré. Her first couple
of poetry books were really well-written, and you could tell
that this person was going to win prizes and be important. But
the nature of her poetry was not all that much different from
other really good descriptive poetry in Canada. It was, for
example, easy to read, with enjoyable images. She developed a
good fan base, as they say in the entertainment business.

But then her poems started getting hard to read. You had to
work to grasp even a bit of them. They were "experimental,"
and "postmodern," and "avant-garde." The fans of her early
work, who wanted more of the same, were unhappy. Oh, Erin,
she was so good, and now she has been kidnapped by all those
far-out crazies.

As to audience: I would be disappointed in myself if all my readers understood everything I was doing. But contrarily, it gives me great pleasure when some ill-dressed twenty-year-old toting a heavy book bag tells me that he caught the recondite reference to Mrs Louis Zukofsky in a short story I wrote. At last, I tell myself.

As to communication: I usually write anyone who writes to me. It may take me a while to get back to them. With e-mail, the situation is simplified. I mean other than dealing with the messages you get from distant highschool kids who have to write an assignment on your work, and they want you to give them some "ideas."

I admire some writing done by writers who claim no political allegiance, and who are then seen to go into back rooms with right-wing thugs — for example, Jorge Luis Borges. I can even read with some pleasure Stalinist assassins such as Pablo Neruda. I admire Roque Dalton, the revolutionary soldier murdered by the Maoists in his own outfit. I can agree with Oscar Wilde's notion that your responsibility is to write well.

Personally, I sympathize with the romantic tolerant left, and in my books you will not find good things said about the USAmerican government, or government by capitalist developers as seen recently in British Columbia. I think that the reader has great social responsibility, that people who shun the news because it is so "depressing" are a waste as human beings. Writers in the world I would like to reside in are not obliged by their talent to try to shape public opinion, but they will occasionally decide to do so. I admire Margaret Atwood for a number of things, and one of them is willingness to speak out and to lend her considerable name to decent causes.

I have politics and I have religion, but I do not look to their standards when I come to write fiction or anything else. I do not work or think, that is, within a political or religious framework. Let us say, rather, that the traces of Christianity left in me will be noticed in my displeasure with USAmerican foreign policy, as seen in my history books. The USA, I believe, is the greatest enemy that Judeo-Christianity has ever had, whether we are talking about the attack on the spirituality of the Bible by those moronic preachers who can only read it literally, as if it had been written by reporters, or the violation of all the Ten Commandments by the USA military in small countries all over the globe.

So am I now talking about religion or politics or social responsibility? I can remember that in Grade 6 my teacher Rudy Guidi was explaining socialism to us, and I thought, well of course that is a logical and emotional extension of Christianity. I still think that. That is why the great preachers of the Canadian prairies were socialists.

*Shakespeare and I*

*First of all I would like to suggest and hope that you* agree, that our modern history cannot in any of its paths be empty of Shakespeare: his presence or his influence. He is there when you wake up in the morning and he is there in every breath you take of the contemporary.

So of course, whenever I retell Canadian history, let us say, in fiction or history texts, Shakespeare is there, doing some of the narrative. Even if I had not read all his plays, he would be there. He would be there a little even if I had not read any of the plays. Well, you know, even the molecules of oxygen he had in his lungs or blood are somewhere in the world right now, maybe inside you.

But I can't quantify how much Shakespeare, that sixteenth-century history reader, has influenced my retelling of Canadian history. I would say that he has not been noticeable to me most of the time while I have been writing, though of course when you are a literary guy writing a novel, say, all kinds of things from your source-pile will find their way in. You will often find me, for instance, quoting Shelley and Keats and so on, usually in the form of quick witty allusions. The Moderns taught us to do that.

All right, Shakespeare is not quantifiable. But both feelings and logic tell us that he is here, in the solution we make our way through. Charles Olson told us that he thought history is located in human thought and action, that it is not a force that sweeps us along, as certain ideologists have maintained. Shakespeare was a human being writing about human beings, not about an age or a world in which human beings were the cyphers. So in my Canadian histories I try to remember and make readers remember that many stories come together to inform us in our place and time. We are not actors in a single all-embracing totalitarian drama staged by an invisible and omnipotent director. When we regard an accident that happens to someone and quote from Shakespeare to respond to it, we are not saying oh look, there is an example of this truism that even Shakespeare knew about. We make connections, not illustrations.

My sense of history is right there. So is my reading of the Bard.

I have published a number of historical novels, and historical poems, and non-fiction history books; and I have written lots of essays that discuss history and its relationships with fiction and other writings. So my wider concept of history is at the same time on record and unclear to me. I am not sure what Shakespeare's theory of history was, though there are probably Shakespeare scholars who can tell us. We certainly have made it our habit to separate his plays into categories — the tragedies, the comedies, the history plays. It seems to me, an amateur, that Shakespeare read accounts of history and fictionalized when it became interesting to do so. I mean when he was not taking other writers' notions and working them 'til they became his own. History, you will remember, is not what transpired but what stories are written about those things that transpired, and remember that those things were available only as stories to begin with. I suppose you could say that I too fictionalize when it becomes interesting to do so. And any reading that anyone does of my writing is of necessity somewhat of a misreading, as is my reading of Shakespeare — but that is another story.

We *take* history, and then perhaps we *give* it. We recognize that things did happen, and we recognize that history is something else, what we in our time think about what might have happened. Professional historians, seeing themselves as scientists, make much of their research, of examining primary materials, as they call them. But those details are usually something someone wrote, somebody's version of what happened.

Just as a nation's story is rather a commingling of stories, so is any one person's view of history. Wordsworth the poet saw himself as a conveyor of the English tradition in poetry, as the latest contributor to the stream fed by Shakespeare and Milton. If such a thing can happen in poetry, it can happen in history. Did you ever notice that half of Shakespeare's plays have Italian settings? Someone once suggested that his father was an immigrant from Italy, and was in the habit of telling Italian stories to William — Romeo and Juliet, Coriolanus, Shylock. I wonder how Shakespeare's father spelled his name in Italian.

So just as the Bard reassembled Italian stories from the air around him, we customarily take stuff from him. We rewrite him, we adapt him, we allude to him, we satirize him, we quote him — even people who don't know what they are borrowing will quote him when they need a cliché to sum up a personal situation. He is that much a part of our story. "Neither a lender nor a borrower be," your uncle will say, having no idea that he is quoting someone who is a figure of fun and pity.

So how could I write a sea story without making reference to Shakespeare's storm and island? I wrote the beginning of *Burning Water* in Trieste, an Italian port city at the north end of Illyria. I wrote the latter part on the Caribbean coast of Costa Rica, where Columbus and his European barques were once moored. For a long time writers have used *The Tempest* as if it belonged to them, as if they were dogs and it was a bone that would never wear out.

(If Shakespeare can take up arms against a sea of troubles, I can surely shift metaphors in mid-stream, so to speak.)

When it came to uttering a selected poems to be published during the year that my sea novel came out, I titled it *Particular Accidents*, a phrase that tersely characterized the way I hoped to compose verse. Of course the phrase was uttered by Prospero to describe the features of the story he will provide to the shipwrecked Italians in Act v, Scene 1. In that same scene he uses the phrase "bring forth a wonder" quite ambiguously, it seems to me. But surely part of the meaning must be to remind us that Prospero the magician and Prospero the story-teller are one. Devotees of the anti-realist novel have long had a soft spot in their heads for *The Tempest*. Part One of *Burning Water* is titled "Bring Forth a Wonder," which was meant to alert readers that there might be a strange music heard from time to time in this book.

On the acknowledgements page appears the warning that the narration of the novel will make use of Shakespeare's fantastic play. Somewhere during the British sailors' voyage they encounter a terrific sea storm, and the author lets William Shakespeare's words describe it. By the late eighteenth century Shakespeare's words had been carried on the wind to the Antipodes. By the late twentieth century they had slipped their way into a Canadian text. If there is such a thing as a "Canadian voice" it is in an air redolent of every language spoken by every poet since light appeared on the new sea.

A European student asked me some years ago: "In reading your novel, it seems to me that while the British 'taught' the Indians their language, the Indians already possessed something more valuable. They had the Great Spirit to grant them their individuality and their identity. Can *Burning Water* be conceived as a re-reading of *The Tempest* in postmodern, postcolonial terms? As a reappropriation of the values the European had tried to erase, without erasing that European overlay?"

I had to say that it would not surprise me nor bother me that an academic might read the book that way. I understood the rise of postcolonial studies when it happened, though I was always a little worried that it seemed to me to be the return of thematic criticism that I thought we had forced back into its lair. As for the Indians, at least those in my book, I don't think that they were that much concerned with individuality or identity. The older of the two main guys always sees those things, as he does the designs of the Great Spirit, with what I think to be welcome irony. There has been, in recent years, a lot of discussion of identity politics in academic studies. When I was a university kid the question of identity always came out of psychology classes or movies about teenagers. I said in those days that my identity could be checked by opening my wallet and looking at the card in there.

But as I have suggested above, there is reason to see a connection between the European-Native situation in *Burning*

*Water* and that in *The Tempest*. I am, being an amateur, uncertain about how ironic Shakespeare was being, but I think that it was quite a lot. When my self-regarding Englishmen (with the exception of Archibald Menzies the botanist) call the native people "treacherous dogs" or "ignorant brute[s]," they do resemble Prospero in the epithets he aims at Prospero (and Ariel). I don't know quite how to read Caliban's remark to his European master in the second scene of the play: "You taught me language, and my profit on 't is, / I know how to curse." But I cannot believe that the European usurper comes off blameless.


One day I was strolling on the seawall with a quiet friend, and we heard another stroller whistling the first movement of the *Fourteenth Quartet in C#*. "That's Beethoven," I said. "That little guy there?" asked my unmusical companion. "No, you see —" I began, but just then another stroller came by, saying quite loudly, "Up with my tent there! Valiant gentlemen, / Let us survey the vantage of the field / Call for some men of sound direction / Let's want no discipline, make no delay, / For, lords, to-morrow is a busy day." I put my fingers to my chin. "Shakespeare," I said. My friend looked back and forth between me and the reciter. "Richard the Third," I said. "Make up your mind," said my companion.

But you see what I mean, don't you. I am not saying that the whistler and the speaker were the nineteenth-century German and the sixteenth-century Brit, but I am not entirely dismissing the fancy. For certain, Beethoven and Shakespeare were there in Stanley Park that sunny afternoon.

Actors have more than once performed *The Tempest* in that park. It is pretty well surrounded by salt water, after all. I don't remember its showing up in *Burning Water*, though it could have. As the "historical" part of that novel takes place at the end of the eighteenth century, I was interested in the early Romantics and their consideration of the relationships among fact, fancy and the imagination. They were concerned with the distinctions to be made between them, and because I was too, I not only stole from them, but also invited them into my story, especially Coleridge and Blake.

But of course Shakespeare is to poetical drama as Beethoven is to European music. Anywhere that Shakespeare has been read, is being read, and will be read, or watched on the stage or on the screen, he will be part of the intellectual history of that place. He is one of those great creators who made and makes a difference all over the world. Whether or not we are aware of it at the time, we writers engage with his mind all the time when we work.

*Thou art alive still while thy book doth live,*
*And we have wits to read and praise to give.*
— BEN JONSON, "To the Memory
of my Beloved the Author,
Mr. William Shakespeare"

*The John & Yoko Tape*

*During the years that I lived in Montréal, 1967 to* 1971, I was the Montréal correspondent for the Vancouver underground weekly, the *Georgia Straight*. I filed stories about Expo, Quebec politics, baseball, burning universities, poetry and music events, exploding mailboxes, and so on. One day I went to interview John Lennon the musician and his partner Yoko Ono the performance artist.

The underground papers were very much interested in the war in Indochina, and in the makers of rock music. When John Lennon the Beatle and his new partner found a unique way to protest the war machine, it was a common-law marriage made in Heaven. John and Yoko had performed a week-long bed-in in Amsterdam. Eventually they would do it in Toronto. In late May of 1969 they rented Room 1742 of the aptly-named Queen Elizabeth Hotel in Montréal, put on white pajamas to match the furnishings, and invited the press to come on up. I didn't have much trouble getting accreditation; Lennon's entourage knew what the *Straight* was.

I have never been the sort of person who has to have the latest gadget. Lately, for example, I have been converting mp3 tunes into CDs. But in 1969, when the cassette tape recorder was pretty new, I went right out and got myself a Philips some-thing-or-other, with the kind of controls you would not see a year later. I bought an 89-cent tape and practised and prac-tised, praying that I would not come back down the elevator with blank cellulose.

By the time I was on the seventeenth floor of the QE, I had the leatherette carrier over my shoulder and the knobby microphone in my right fist. The way it worked was that the downstairs handlers would let in a handful of interviewers at a time. Luckily, I was in a tiny group of three. One was a rather shy lad, probably from a college paper, and the other was a jerk from a local newspaper who thought that rock and anti-war activity were not serious enough for honest attention.

Here are two impressions I retain from my visit. John Len-non seemed like an ordinary good-hearted guy with the same Liverpool accent you heard in the movies. And Yoko Ono was beautiful, far more attractive than she ever was in photo-graphs and film. I am a little embarrassed to admit that when our twenty minutes were up and it was time to go, I patted the bespectacled rock star on the top of his head.

I transcribed part of the interview and published it in the *Straight*. Forty years later I sent the tape to a London auction house. I was raising money for some dental surgery.

*Lyric, Experiment, Conservatives*

*A few years back, after the publication of a big collec-*tion of poems called *Vermeer's Light*, I did a reading tour of New York state, finishing in Buffalo, an important place in the history of the new poetry, where I got into a conversation with Geoffrey Hlibchuk and others. They wanted me to clarify my sentiments about this and that, so I gave it a try.

As a way of warming up, they asked me whether, given the recent big changes in my life, there were any particular pressures on me in the writing and publishing of this book. I said that there weren't any real pressures other than the usual chance that the muse and my friends might disapprove. So far, so good.

There is the curious fact that I don't do poetry collections as frequently as I used to. Maybe no one does. Long ago I might do one every three years, and there might be a book-length poem between them. This Vermeer one was the first in ten years, and before that the gap was about five years. I guess I am just not as eager as I used to be. You will see that most of the poems in these two hundred pages are parts of something a little larger, a series, or a little book, such as the twenty-six page *A, You're Adorable* by Ellen Field, my faithful *nom d'informatique*. In my youth I was writing lyric poems all the time, on cigarette packages and bookmarks. Now they come to me, but I don't often bother writing them down.

Maybe you could say that the lyric poems I do bother to write down are often tangled with historical, social or nationalist concerns. That would probably point to my ambivalent attitude towards the lyric form. As with so many things, here I am of two minds. There are two main features of the lyric poem, right? It is musical and it is individual, personal. I will never be resistant to the musical, as certain language poets are, but I do believe that the personal can be a great bore, as it so often turns out to be with "confessional" poets. My tutor Robert Duncan could be said to have retained the musical and found a way out of the personal. La la. He was always insistent on the song that is to be found in language. There was some music that he didn't know much about. Once at a house party in Vancouver he said that he was going to experiment with jazz bits. Knowing Robert, I squinched up my face and asked him what he meant. Oh, you know, he said, Noel Coward, that sort of thing.

Someone wrote recently that I was doing something unusual by constructing long poems with the lyric running through them. Could be. There are some strictly lyric poets practicing now that are really good. First one thinks of Sharon Thesen. But her one long poem didn't work out very well. So listen: couldn't you say that Lorene Niedecker was a great lyric poet? Isn't James Schuyler among other things a great lyric voice? Even bpNichol, who is celebrated for his concrete poems and his anti-narrative devices, has more lyrical inclinations than some readers are willing to admit.

That said, I think it's safe to say that *Vermeer's Light* often aims to transcend the lyric. Naturally, in Buffalo they wanted to know whether as a lyric poet I could define my relationship with experimentation. Or to put it another way, if someone enjoys being some kind of established poet, where would an inclination toward the experimental come from? I wanted to know whether they were referring to bpNichol or to me. Ellen Field does mention in her poem that bpNichol is her favourite poet, and as Ms Field has now been revealed to be another me, I guess you could say that at least while I was being Ellen Field, Mr Nichol was my favourite poet. I don't know whether I really do have a favourite poet, I said, or whether I keep on having the same favourite poet. At the moment, I said, my favourite USAmerican poet was Ron Padgett, but that could change the next time I took to reading something great by Rae Armantrout.

Get off the pot, they said.

All right. I recently published a short story that was titled "An Experimental Story" because it was developed in the structure of a highschool chemistry experiment, with hypothesis, materials, quantitative data and all those headings. In the tangle of terms people use to talk about contemporary writing, I don't mind the term "experimental," as long as it does not just refer to something out of the ordinary, as long as the writer is clearly conducting an experiment, with the knowledge that a majority of experiments will fail, that the hypotheses will be unsatisfied.

I will tell you about one of mine that failed. For years I planned to pretend that the word "canto" rather than the word "camera" means "room" in Italian. Then I planned to invent a guy who will wander from "room" to "room" in Ezra Pound's *Cantos*. Eventually I set to work. I tried and tried, and it just did not work. That was neither the first nor the last experiment I would clean up after without a positive conclusion.

Experimental or not, the unconventional has always interested me. That's why I was so happy to have my linguistics
professor Ron Baker introduce me to Oulipo. That is why I
felt so lucky to have a girlfriend whose stepmother was Barbara Pentland, the far-out composer. That's why I recognized
the painter Greg Curnoe as my brother when I lived for a year
in London, Ont.

Now the Buffalo people took a turn that surprised me.
Hlibchuk said, "As a Canadian poet with a heightened aware-
ness of history and American culture (and I'm reminded here
of your friendships with politically-minded writers like Ginsberg and Olson), has the recent upsurge in American neo-
conservatism played any part in your consciousness as a poet?
Or as a writer in general?"

I had just been in the USA for a week, happily in what I
imagine to be a Democratic sector, though I have noticed that
if you drive a non-turnpike highway across the northern part
of New York, you will see that every nice white-painted house
in every little town has a big USA flag in front of it.

USAmerican neo-conservatism is perhaps the saddest story
of my life, because when I was a kid I swallowed all that guff
about the USA as a beacon to the world, as the home of dem-
ocracy and forward-looking governments and so on. I read a
lot of comic books, and I listened to a lot of USAmerican radio
stations. But as I grew up I studied USA history at university,
and kept reading about public life, as we are encouraged to do
as democratic people. And I learned that the USA is a country
that has to be dragged kicking and screaming into modern
reforms or current centuries. It was one of the last places to
make slavery illegal, and then it said okay to Jim Crow. It is
one of the last remaining places to continue killing prisoners.
When there is a war against fascism it enters the war halfway

through, but when there are left-leaning governments elected in Latin America, it overthrows them violently as quickly as possible. It hangs on to miles and pounds and Fahrenheit when the rest of the world has thrown them out along with furlongs and cubits and the like. It allows health care and hospitalization to be conducted on a business model.

The problem with the neo-conservatives is that they render progress, catching up with the world, harder to achieve. They make ignorance powerful, and make hate groups such as the Moral Majority or the Tea Party influential. USAmericans sometimes refer to "the left." A lot of Republicans actually refer to President Obama as a "socialist." In most of the world he would be seen as right of centre.

As to the effect of this sad story on my writing? I have despaired of satire. Satire requires an audience that is intelligent enough to see what one is doing, and a hope that it can do some good. The people nurtured on cell-phone socializing will not know how to read satire. In some dictatorships it is a crime to be a satirist. In other places, where the people have lost touch with the principles that started their civilization, satire gets hidden behind the search, for example, for an "American Idol."

Whew. I said all that to a group of USAmericans. Fortunately, I was in Buffalo, New York rather than Midland, Texas. I remember that Jean got me out of Midland, Texas as soon as the ball game was over. In Texas we ate roadside picnics so that I wouldn't get into political discussions in restaurants or bars. Buffalo is another matter. Quite a few of my writing friends went to Buffalo because it was a new writing hub in the sixties and seventies. I go to Buffalo once a year or so, to sit in the Anchor Bar with my friend Jack, or to read some pages in a university hall or bookstore.

Next my Buffalo interviewers wanted to know whether I have any special memories of Buffalo.

I would not say that I have spectacular memories of Buffalo. Once a bunch of us hip young Canadian poets put on a show over several days at a long straight house designed by Frank Lloyd Wright. One day a couple of years ago I was driving through downtown Buffalo, looking for a way to get to the bridge to Ontario (or as they say down there, "Canada") and got snarled in a lot of contradictory construction and signage. A Buffalo cop told me to get out of the country. Then he pointed the way. My thanks to him. I like to go to Bisons games (baseball) when I can make it. The first time was on a cold night but my friend Jack had brought a huge thermos full of hot tea, apparently a Buffalo ritual. When we drank it in the stands it tasted a little like something else, or maybe tea tastes different on the Niagara Frontier.

In late 1966 or early 1967 I drove from London, Ontario to Buffalo to attend a reading by Anselm Hollo, the first time I had seen him since the previous summer in London, England. Buffalo was hopping then, threatening to take the governorship of poetry away from Vancouver. John Wieners was there, and he had a tooth. I went to the Anchor Bar and ate real wings, thereby becoming familiar with one of the two places that hold out a promise of redemption for the USA, the other being the Tampico Mexican restaurant in Everett, Washington.

# Digging Up Dundas

Commencement address at
University of Western Ontario, May 2003

*In 1966, long before most of you were born — heck,* before some of your professors were born — I fulfilled a dream and came to London, Ontario to be a university student. I hadn't dreamt about being a university student. It was just that in 1954 when I was on the basketball team of the RCAF station at Borden, we had made a visit to London. They were digging up Dundas Street, but I still liked the look of the place and said I would like to live there one day, and now in 1966, here I was, and they were digging up Dundas Street.

My friend Greg Curnoe, the great painter, said that I should have been there in 1964. They weren't digging up Dundas Street in 1964.

So far this is a pointless story.

I spent the long snowy winter of 1966–67 at the University of Western Ontario, taking graduate courses. I was going to try to become the first PhD in English at Western. So I quit writing poems and stories for a while, and concentrated on Walt Whitman and Percy Bysshe Shelley. I did not go to one pep rally or football game or beer meeting at some mysterious hotel beverage room called "the Ceeps." I concentrated.

Outside of school I sat up 'til four in the morning, learning about art and music from Greg Curnoe, and pretending that I was enamoured of a peculiar London, Ontario orchestra called the Nihilist Spasm Band. Greg had flunked out of art school; he derisively called me "Doctor Bowering." In fact, I think that was the title of the portrait he drew of me the day before we left London for Montréal.

That would be my ultimate trip to Montréal. My previous trip took place in February, when I was invited to Sir George Williams University to do a poetry reading. They put us up, my wife Angela and me, in the Ritz-Carlton Hotel. They took us out to a lavish dinner before the reading, and after the reading they threw me a fancy party. The SGWU reading series of 1966–71 was the best reading series there has ever been at a Canadian university.

I am beginning to perceive the possibility that this story may have a point, but so far I could not tell you what it might be.

Anyway, Montréal, eh? By 1966–67 I had come to know quite a bit about the recent history of Canadian poetry, and the part that had occurred in Montréal was very glamorous, even before Leonard Cohen showed up.

So what was I going to do when in the spring of 1967 the people who had invited me to do a reading in their super reading series now telephoned me and asked whether I might want to come to Montréal and be the writer in residence at Sir George Williams University. But gosh, I had a year of residency to put in at Western, and a thesis to write.

But you see, I was thirty-one years old. It was Canada's centenary year, and there was all that glamour. I will put the choice to Angela, I decided: Montréal or London? London or

Montréal? I knew what was going on when I saw her carrying a book called *The Cooking of Urban Quebec.*

So we went to Montréal and took part in all that glamour, and I never did finish my PhD studies. Western offered me a really good deal regarding scholarships and so on, but though we would come back to visit Greg Curnoe and his family, I never did write that PhD thesis.

Am I ever glad that I got into the university game in the Sixties! Just try getting a good university job now without a PhD. Well, my MA wasn't all that great, either. I never wrote my doctoral thesis, but I did find time to write a lot of books. And for some reason my university, Simon Fraser, kept giving me promotions.

I always said that getting a PhD would be bad for my career — as a poet, that is. But I always felt a little as if I had let the University of Western Ontario down. They had made space for me. They had taught me a lot, especially about Shelley. They had provided a chocolate bar machine in Huron College that, if you lifted it by the corner and dropped it gently, you could get a free chocolate bar.

So when Western asked me whether I would come and be writer in residence here, thirty-seven years after being lured away by a similar invitation, I said sure. Then I had a great idea: how about it if I were to finish my PhD studies while I was here being writer in residence? I could get my old poetry pal Dr Frank Davey to be my supervisor. Maybe I could be my own external examiner.

I think that was when the idea surfaced to offer me an honorary degree at UWO. It would save everyone a lot of work and embarrassment. It would mean that instead of writing a thesis, I could write a novel filled with bright images and sly allusions. It would be, I can tell you, a very welcome honour from the school that I spent too short a time at.

And I will admit that while I did not go to the Ceeps, I did manage to spend quite a lot of time at the York.

I am not so sure that I am going to make a point here. This sounds like autobiography. The only other time I got an honorary degree I wrote a piece called "Laughing at Grads," and you can look that up if you have a completely idle afternoon sometime in this career you are now aimed at.

I have listened to a few graduation addresses from honored guests and valedictorians, and here is one thing I have noticed: they are all about making a point. Graduation day is really important to families. Look at all the cameras. It is the end of something — this, say your parents, is what we have been looking forward to since the first time you threw up while we were burping you. It is also the beginning of something — this is where the clichés are supposed to rain down. You are opening a door to a future in an uncertain world that demands the whole works from your generation. Don't worry: you won't remember anything about this next week.

But look how lucky I am. Today, while you are waiting 'til you can get those funny clothes off, I am enjoying something that seems to go on all my life. This is not the beginning of something, and it is not the end of something. It is not all over; it is over all. I really appreciate what I am being given. And this is my point, after all. I hope that it happens to you, too. I hope that getting your degree does not mean the end of your youth or the beginning of your job. I hope that this day lasts you your whole lifetimes. Even when some day you can't remember who the heck was talking to you on graduation day, you might say as I am saying to myself today: "Is this ever neat!"

*Al Purdy*

# Al and Me

*For decades I have been asking myself the question:* what is it about Al Purdy and me? I was the first person to write a book about Al Purdy. I have published several long articles about him, a number of memoirs, lots of poems, and reviews of at least half his books. I made him a character in a novel, for heaven's sake. I arranged for appearances by Purdy at four universities. I carried on a correspondence with him for forty years. We did tandem readings at universities, libraries, and art galleries. We got our pictures taken together more often than Wayne and Schuster.

Now that my wife has started a campaign to save Al and Eurithe Purdy's bucolic A-frame house in eastern Ontario, I find myself spending every day with the late poet. And I wonder how come.

Because what did Alfred Wellington Purdy and George Harry Bowering have in common? He came from a kind of rural area near the centre of the universe, and I grew up in a desert valley way out near the western edge. When it came time to approach poetry and the writing of same, our differences were not simply a matter of age. Al was seventeen years older than I, but my mentor Robert Duncan was only a few months younger than Al.

The divergence shows up in the names of the precedent poets we took to mentioning. Al referred to the Brits G.K. Chesterton and Hilaire Belloc, whereas I cited the USAmerican figures William Carlos Williams and H.D. Did this mean that our sensibilities were British vs. USAmerican? Not at all. I think that we are all agreed that Al was about as Canadian as you can get in the public eye, in the same way that his favourite singer Stan Rogers was. Singer and poet both reached for the Beaufort Sea, as robust Ontario Canadians will do.

Purdy is famous for his depiction of the place so strenuously celebrated in the recent *A-Frame Anthology*, little Roblin Lake and the scant village of Ameliasburgh, old United Empire Loyalist land in Prince Edward County. You see those proper nouns? When the tall, big-elbowed poet celebrates a region, he hauls the whole of his country with him. One of his last major poems, "Say the Names," strides across that country, naming its historical and mythological places, with the undisguised intent of celebrating a whole country, an abstraction to be made tangible to the expansive Canadian mind. In that poem he insists that you speak the musical names aloud, including those from my home, Osoyoos and Similkameen.

From the beginning of my serious poetry life I too have been interested in place. Here, though, is our difference on this matter. Purdy loves his place, and gathers it to his self, so much so that he will be identified with it, become in time our most famous Canadian poet. I, on the other hand, have been tentative in verse, Purdy's opposite in that regard maybe, finding any connection with my place via my physical senses, perceiving my Okanagan ground and my body with the same procedure.

Al will say, "I am a screen thru which the world passes."

I will say, "The white wolf hides in the snow."

O, how we argued in our letters, or I argued while Al disputed, refuted, pronounced, and expounded. Al was from United Empire Loyalist country, don't forget, so he felt that if he had to appreciate me it was despite my association with such USAmerican poets as Robert Creeley and Charles Olson. For UEL Al, the war that the USAmericans called a revolution was not over or forgiven. He thought that John Newlove had what it takes. I imagine too that he forgave Newlove for carrying Wallace Stevens's collected poems wherever he went. Clearly Stevens the insurance company employee was closer to being Canadian than was Olson the USAmerican Democratic Party apparatchik.

Everyone who shares a history with Al Purdy knows that he loved to provoke some kind of disagreement. He would play the devil's advocate long after the devil had dispensed with his services. In my head at this moment I can hear his distinctive sea lion voice offering me the opportunity to beg a question I had no intention to beg. "Wouldn't you say that Dorothy Livesay's later poetry was really newspaper prose because of her broken love affair with a Jewish Lithuanian air cadet girl?" No, Al. Not really newspaper prose, I would maintain, and there'd be that grin with a toothpick in it on a face also concerned with tilting back and accepting a glug out of a stubby of whatever beer was at the time the most economical to purchase.

But you know, while all this game-playing was going on, one was spending an afternoon and evening enjoying oneself, the company one had fallen among, and the things one found out one knew at last. Do you see? So one would eventually get out onto the 401 Highway, glowing a bit, and would the poet and his wife be left all alone in those woods? No, Al Purdy was a famous collector of books, and he read them too, during those cold nights when he and the missus sat and saw themselves reflected in the lakeshore window set into the abode they'd built out of second-hand lumber because they had to.

I like to picture Al reading my first book at Roblin Lake. Because there is a similarity to offset our differences. Our "break-through" books were published by Contact Press. Contact Press was the first really important Canadian poetry publisher to emerge in the years after the Second World War. It was a small press in the best sense, producer of plain and attractive objects that were also the first significant poetry books by the next wave of Canadian poets, a wave that followed pretty calm waters, one might say. Its founders and first editors were Irving Layton, Louis Dudek, and Raymond Souster, with Souster doing the majority of the work.

Contact Press would release volumes by Milton Acorn, Margaret Atwood, D.G. Jones, John Newlove, Frank Davey, Gwendolyn MacEwen, Alden Nowlan, and Lionel Kearns, among others. Al Purdy, if he knew, may have had to overlook the fact that the press was named in honour of an earlier small press created by William Carlos Williams, among others. Al's famous friend Milton Acorn would spend later years bemoaning the influence of the USAmerican "Black Mountain poets," and perhaps regret that he had dedicated his Contact Press book to one of them.

In 1962 Contact Press published Al's *Poems for all the Annettes*, and in the small world of Canadian literature the 43-year-old Purdy was all at once the hot new item. Or at least that's the way I looked at it from my borrowed chair out on the west coast, where I was the oldest of the editors who had started *Tish*, the contentious poetry newsletter, a year earlier. I knew that Al was not exactly the sort of thing we'd found in the New York and San Francisco magazines we were reading, and there was a danger that the Irving Layton bluff might have rubbed off on him during his days in Montréal's poetry kitchen. But *Poems for all the Annettes* showed me a composer no longer willing to assemble quatrains of end-rime and other Imperial restraints. His poems were starting to scatter across the pages, a little obviously, maybe, but at least as if they were trying to enact perception rather than glorifying personality the way Layton did. At least that's the way this 26-year-old on the coast saw it:

> And I can't make it be
> what it isn't by saying,
> or take the shape of a word's being.

My friends the *Tish* poets warned me. They said look out for bluster. They noticed a little bluster in me and warned against it even if it was supposed to be a kind of hip bluster. I said we need friends in the east. They said the east doesn't get it. I used all the influence I could exert at the University of British Columbia, where I was supposed to be a graduate student, and got Al his first reading there. I wrote pieces for the campus newspaper about the hottest new thing in Canadian Literature. I reviewed *Poems for all the Annettes* in *Tish* and the *Ubyssey*. By the time that Al showed up we had become friends through the mail. One of my heroes from *The New American Poetry* was teaching at UBC that year. He got drunk at a party and tried to sock me. He was concerned that with all this Purdy business I hadn't accurately or bravely listened to my proper muse.

*Annettes* really was a breakthrough book for Al. Pretty soon he was a McClelland & Stewart poet (back when that meant something) and publishing clothbound books that won him readers and prizes and at least a place in the pantheon alongside Irving Layton and Earle Birney. Now he could forget about writing tedious radio plays and gather a big Canada Council grant, and this is where he made the smart move that would steer him towards fame as Canada's two-fisted and sure-hearted proto-national poet. In the sixties, Canadian writers and painters were spending their Canada Council grants in sunny Spain or Greece. Not Purdy. He hitched a ride to Canada's eastern Arctic.

The result was a semi-coffeetable book called *North of Summer*, with oil sketches by A.Y. Jackson, Canada's most famous living artist. Jack McClelland told me that he'd told Jackson that Purdy's poems would be there as company for the paintings, and told Al that Jackson's paintings were there to illustrate his book of poems. Whatever it was, here was a book to please anyone, catching the wave of centenary patriotism while offering humorous and dramatic vignettes of life in a place that could be nothing other than Canadian. Purdy's Pangnirtung had trumped Layton's Attica and Birney's Macchu Picchu.

I liked *North of Summer* because it was not a hodgepodge, because it was written and edited as a *book*, a series of poems written as parts of a larger attention. In Canada, collections of occasional verse were the norm. Louis Dudek and James Reaney were the only major poets who conceived books as verse sequences. I looked forward to more such excursions by my non-mentor.

But while slightly younger poets such as Phyllis Webb and Roy Kiyooka were starting to write sequences and serial poems, Purdy became the wild grape-wine bard, creating a persona that would make him popular outside the cloistered world of Canlit. He turned out a large number of good poems, many of them set in beer parlours and his sylvan bedroom, many others along the trails of his exotic travels, from Moscow to the Galápagos Islands. No longer would we see and thus hear a curious intelligence searching for form, but rather a learned and confident rascal who found it natural to offer observations and authority in a fully persuasive Canadian vernacular. The poems filled a page or two with lines strung just this side of musical prose, and people, as they say, ate them up.

I enjoyed buying and reading every book as it appeared from McClelland & Stewart and then from Howard White's fine Harbour Publishing, which would eventually publish Purdy's huge collected poems and now the *A-Frame Anthology*. I also appreciated Al's sending me signed copies of the odd ephemeral publications he did so many of in his last decades. But by now I knew that Al Purdy and I were old-time friends, not co-religionists in verse. Fine — once that was out of the way, we could bluster into one another's lives, a couple of guys who knew what most people were missing.


An adjective often applied to Al Purdy was "rawboned." When it came from a delicate aesthete or well-cooked academic, it might seem a little condescending. On the other hand, it apparently gave a legion of self-declared "people's poets" license to declare Al their bardic father, without their finding it necessary to do a fiftieth of the reading that he did.

This is where poets and friends talk about the last time they saw Al. My daughter Thea and I went to the Purdys' sea-side house on Vancouver Island about a week before Al died in April 2000. Al was in jammies and a robe, with one of those oxygen feeders in his nostrils, and sitting in a wheelchair. He'd just got out of bed to say hello. Despite all this stuff he still looked rawboned. And he still had a lot of that sea lion voice so many Canadian poets like to do impressions of. He used it now for a purpose I was glad to hear.

"Ahhhh, Bowering," he said, "What's the most you ever got paid for one poem?"

"Oh, I don't know, maybe two hundred simoleons," I replied, trying to remember whether I was exaggerating.

He pounced.

"Ha! I just got $2,500 for a poem in the *Imperial Oil Review*," he said, with his usual air of provocation. So close to what was coming. How I loved him then, even loving the way he made me feel a little embarrassed even while he was not at all so. This was the lifelong strategy of an essentially shy person more famous than he secretly thought he was.

A year later, Al's wife Eurithe told me that Al added a hundred dollars every time he told that story. I might have added a hundred just now.

# The Al Frame

*Tuesday, May 16, 1967 was a warm sunny centenary* year day in what people kept telling me was eastern Ontario. I was driving a maroon Chevy with too many miles on it, on my way from London, Ontario, where I lived at the time in what people told me was western Ontario, though the vast majority of Ontario is west of it, to Montréal, where I would give a poetry reading at a downtown university and, what was then unknown to me, be examined as a candidate for their writer-in-residence job.

I am saying that when I lived in British Columbia, I situated myself by place, its directions and roadways. In Ontario there was no hope of understanding the place. That is so partly because the people there live in history rather than geography. And they tend to mean Ontario when they say Canada. So, Al Purdy, we tend to mean Canada when we say Purdy. I turned off the 401, the Macdonald-Cartier Highway (you see what I mean?), looking for the fabled hamlet of Ameliasburgh, or as Al Purdy spelled it, "Ameliasburg," while he was providing its fable. In the Chevy with me were my wife Angela, a pain-in-the-ass hippy wannabe from Calgary whose name was Ron, my chihuahua dog Frank, and Frank's little chihuahua, Small.

Here's what it says in my diary: "On the way up [or down, as it is called there] we stayed overnight at Purdy's famous A-frame house in Ameliasburg, where we had stew and booze and late talk, and in the morning as we were lugging stuff to the car the rural-type assessor arrived as Ron came out with his bells around his neck, and Purdy in his shorts."

An appalling image, but one we all hold dear.

I might have been lost in Ontario, but I knew my way around Al Purdy's poetry in 1967, and I was enjoying myself the way some Wordsworth scholars must feel when they moon over the lake country. There was the church steeple, there was the home-made house, there was the "lake," and there was the wife, Eurithe: "and while that white body protrudes / over on my side of the bed / pride is damn difficult . . ." The little dogs loved it at Roblin Lake, and so did we.

When Angela in her short skirt climbed to look at the loft we would sleep in eventually, Al the perfect host held the ladder and watched to make sure that she didn't slip. When she went to use the outhouse, he manfully flung the door open so I could get a picture for, uh, posterity. She would notice that Al was partly concealed by some leafy branches, and labeled the snap "Al the Faun." In our late night discussion of poetics, Al said "bullshit" twenty-one times and I said "horseshit" eighteen times. Al always won those debates.

In 1967 the Purdys' house was nearly alone on that big pond, and what with old wheelbarrow and upside-down rowboat and empty stubbies in the unshorn grass out front, it all seemed to this innocent westerner a kind of dilapidated eastern elegance, a kind of dogpatch resort, something nicer than I would ever have in my un-airconditioned big city apartments. When Al brought out an old tome full of plot maps for the local Prince Edward County farms given to United

Empire Loyalists a century and a half before, he was doing me a favour. Maybe he knew that I was going to write my book about him — I don't know.

I don't remember how many times I have been to the Al-frame. In the early eighties Brian Fawcett was going to visit Montréal for the first time, so I went along with him to show him around. We turned off the 401 to see whether the Purdys were home, but they must have been in Ecuador or Turkmenistan or some such place, so we just looked around the county, with all its old shiny grey wood fences and so on. I noticed that there were by then a few more houses, or as they call them in Ontario, cottages around Roblin Lake.

Early in the new century Jean Baird and I were driving back south (west) on the 401, after some poetry stuff in Montréal, and halfway between Kingston and Belleview we took a quick glance at each other and smiled, and whoever was driving turned off for Purdy country. Jean Baird and Eurithe Purdy have been comparing notes for years, and on this occasion we got lucky — Eurithe had arrived at the A-frame that very day. I can't remember whether we coaxed her down from the roof, but we sure had a good visit.

I was a little disconcerted to see that the lake is now surrounded by cottages, but that's how Ontario has changed over the past half century. Grey Owl would have to put up with the generator noise from the next tent if he were schlepping beavers that day. But those two energetic Ontario women did have a nice surprise for me. Sometime late in the twentieth century the locals had named a backcountry road for their poet, and Al was amused by the fact that Purdy Lane leads down to the riverside graveyard. That is where Eurithe and Jean took me, to see Al's remarkable headstone, a big black shiny book with the author's name on the spine. Terrific, eh?

# The Poetry Cottage
## in Prince Edward County

*I will arise and go now, and go to Innisfree,*
*And a small cabin build there, of clay and wattles made*

**W.B. Yeats was one of Al Purdy's favourite poets, and** Al often quoted or misquoted "The Lake Isle of Innisfree." However, when it came to building a place beside a lake, he gave no thought to clay and wattles, but rather cadged or liberated second-hand boards from demolition sites, and built one of the most interesting cottages still standing in Prince Edward County. When he started the cabin he was an unknown and plain mediocre poet. A few years later, he won his first Governor-General's Award in poetry and became the unofficial poet laureate of the whole country.

Roblin Lake, named for Owen Roblin, a flour-mill owner and United Empire Loyalist, is a superannuated pond in the middle of Prince Edward County, an irregular splat of land hanging off the torso of Upper Canada and almost floating away into eastern Lake Ontario. In 1957, Al Purdy, the failed poet, was living with his wife, Eurithe, in the house of his mother in nearby Trenton, where he had dropped out of high school partway through Grade 10. He and Eurithe had a thousand and some dollars somehow saved from their scrabbly jobs in Montréal, and they were looking for a way to live cheaply while Al made them a living by writing plays for the CBC. A site was available for $800 on a corner of Roblin Lake, and they snapped it up. Now they had a few hundred dollars left, and no house.

Like so many other things in their lives, the Purdys' cottage started in a magazine. In his autobiography, *Reaching for the Beaufort Sea*, Al writes that they came across a copy of *House Beautiful* that featured pictures of an A-frame that anyone with an opposable thumb could put together. I think he just figured that the magazine name he used was funny, given his circumstances. In actuality, they were looking at the June 1957 issue of *Canadian Homes and Gardens*, which was subtitled "12 Summer Cottages." The cover featured a dramatically posed and glassy A-frame and the promise "You can build this cottage for $2,000." Al and Eurithe did not have $2,000, but they went daily to their little bit of paradise and began the unglamorous work of turning a sloping and willow-tangled plot into something flat enough to put a floor onto. And they sent away 12 more of their dollars for the A-frame plans, as prepared by the eminent architect Leo Venchiarutti.

From the beginning, Eurithe Purdy, who had worked as a secretary, but who had to figure out how a hammer worked, was at least her husband's equal when it came to labour and endurance and sense. Together they moiled on that lake shore, and eventually there was some flat ground they measured with string. They did not keep track of the number of swear words and epithets. Now if they only had some building materials, they could start this adventure in what has come to be called "vernacular architecture." Did I just hear Al Purdy laughing somewhere?

I was a boy in the Okanagan Valley in the 1950s, so I didn't really know what a cottage was. A cottage, I learned by reading poetry, was something that William Wordsworth wrote poems in, situated in what the Brits called "the Lake Country." Then I heard that it was a place that middle-class Torontonians went to in the summer, either down by the lake or up in Muskoka.

So, I figured, cottages are next to lakes, and you can write poems in them.

Where I come from, a few people might have had a cabin somewhere in the mountains. Back in town it would have been called a one-room shack. It was not until the late twentieth century, when Central Canadian professors came to teach on the west coast and thought they needed a summer place on one of the Gulf Islands, that we got cottages. But by then I had seen cottages in Ontario.

The first I ever saw was one used by a bunch of London, Ontario artists in a strange little place called Grand Bend on Lake Huron. They were Greg Curnoe and his lot, members of the artists' anti-music ensemble, the Nihilist Spasm Band. They called their place No Haven. I suppose that I was still thinking "cabin," but I was a little surprised when I got there. What they called a "cottage" was a house, and it was on a street with other houses, and nearby was a strip of gaudy hot dog stands and circus rides. But I had just moved to Southwest Ontario and had to learn the language. A cottage was a house near a lake that was a drive's distance from Toronto. A one-storey house, someone told me. But in the Okanagan all the houses were one-storey.

There are no hot dog stands anywhere near Roblin Lake.

Ameliasburgh — a smattering of buildings a kilometre across the lake — is the rural part of rural eastern Ontario. If you read Purdy's autobiography and early Ameliasburgh poems, you will read that Purdy was a "sallow-complexioned" exile from the big city. But if you ask Eurithe, she will tell you that she was small-town (Belleville) and he was even smaller-town (Trenton). Luckily, small-town guys know how to saw a straight line, and they tend to know enough people who will tell them where some second-hand lumber might be found.

When I walk around inside the A-frame now, I hear myself saying, "I couldn't have done this." I helped my dad build our house in the Okanagan, but I am just amazed that the Purdys put this place up starting in the cold winter of 1957–58. When Purdy's first Ameliasburg poems were published, the Canadian poetry world felt just as amazed. And numerous commentators have said that both the building and the poetry were constructed with a happy makeshift vision. Forget any clay and wattles — think boards hauled from a demolished building in Belleville. As the years go by and extensions and outbuildings are added, think boards from a CPR freight car, think the floor from the Anne Street School, think Al's mother's house — when Trenton decided to widen its streets, the front porch on her house had to come off. It is now doing duty as a few interior walls at Roblin Lake.

They got help. This was what the local road signs call The County, after all. Eurithe's father lent a hand and a truck. While reading a couple of Al's poems, you might get the impression that the poet Milton Acorn paid rent and board by sawing and hammering. The more reliable myth is that Eurithe hammered nails while Acorn and Purdy argued about ancient Greek history.

While ice covered the lake, the brave pair and their son,

Jimmy, made it through that first winter in the 17-by-30-foot
A-frame with the little kitchen attached. They had a small
woodstove to take care of the four rooms, and groceries that
were found in much the same way that the building materials
were. As the years went by they added a little tool shed–writing room out back, a garage–guesthouse that would later burn
down, and in the seventies a 14-by-28-foot addition to the A-
frame, making a new kitchen and a big dining–living room.
This space boasts the first tailor-made boards in the building,
long planks cut from trees on someone's farm up north and
made into a beautiful ceiling that the six-foot-three Al Purdy
could touch. Touch and own and look on with satisfaction.

> On a green island in Ontario
> I learned about being human
> built a house and found the woman
> and we shall be there forever
> building a house that is never finished

And so it seems. Like just about every Canadian poet I
know, I visited the ongoing project, and had some stew Eurithe made and a stubby of "golden flowers" Al put in my hand.
I came first in 1967, then about once a decade, until the fall of
2010, when I sat and rested, or washed my hair and brushed
my teeth with lake water, while Eurithe and my wife, Jean
Baird, did an inventory of the whole shebang. Jean is leading
the effort to save the A-frame as a writers' retreat, fighting off
the developers who would love to convert that treasure into
a teardown. In the days we spent there, the house was full of
people. But that's nothing new.

Shortly after we arrived, another car came down the almost
invisible grassy driveway. It contained a young woman who

had recently studied Canadian literature and, like so many others, was ravaged by Al Purdy's poems. She just wanted to look around the yard, maybe, look across the lake at the famous church steeple in one of Al's poems. Eurithe, as she had done countless times before, asked her in to look around, and struck up a conversation. When the happy young woman had signed the guest book and driven away, Eurithe told us that the day before she had been visited by a group of fifty bicyclists.

All day there were knocks at the door. Librarians, teachers, plumbers, in-laws, UEL descendants, good citizens from the County arrived to lend a hand, try a new idea, find out more about the A-Frame Trust, and tell the delighted Ms Baird how much Ameliasburgh and the environs were animated by the idea of saving a cottage. In Canada there are a lot of rubble piles that used to be the homes of painters and writers and even architects. Al Purdy's legendary cottage is unlike any other. It was built by the poet himself. It is a rare surviving example of the alternative homes put up by amateurs in the fifties and sixties. It is the site where a pretty bum rhymester turned into a masterful national poet. But it would not matter if the joists were made of the True Cross and Noah's Ark — there'd still be a developer not far away who would like to set a bulldozer on it and put up a piece of gracious living in its place. A piece of prose.

But Ms Baird and the A-Frame Trust have been gathering momentum, and people all over the country have been springing to the defence of Purdy's Folly. Poets, musicians, academics, foundations, booksellers, fast-food executives, farmers, fishermen, and friends have been cutting cheques. People who will never see the A-frame have sent their wages. Poets who had the fortune to sleep in the A-frame's loft have mailed in their support. And what about the citizens of Ameliasburgh and Prince Edward County and environs? There's the great news.

There was a time when the Purdys could toil in anonymity on their side of the lake, even remain unseen while chopping through the ice to get cooking water. But the poetry kept getting better, and the village kept getting more famous, and the cars full of poets kept coming through the village looking for the cottage on Gibson Road. Ameliasburgh is a backwater's backwater, but it is just the kind of community that found it perfectly fine to accommodate a big raw-boned galoot who split his time between bottling wild-grape wine and scrawling poems about Owen Roblin, the most prominent name in the graveyard beside his old millpond.

So that when it came to celebrating its celebrity, as small burgs like to do, Ameliasburgh named a lane after him. Al was amused by the fact that Purdy Lane led down to the graveyard. It is now called Purdy Street, and you can follow it down to the beautiful book-shaped stone with Al Purdy's name on it, not many steps from Owen Roblin's resting place.

Since Al's death in 2000, the village and county have embraced him as their favourite son. Even while he was still alive, the little library at the end of the main street bore his name, and inside it you will find a collection of Purdy stuff, including the ribbons and medals commemorating his inductions into the Order of Canada and Order of Ontario. You won't find these things in many cottage areas.

When a poet lives and writes in lake country, his songs reply to the songs that nature brings him. That's what happened to

William Wordsworth in his lake country, as told in his poem
"The Ruined Cottage":

> A linnet warbled from those lofty elms,
> A thrush sang loud, and other melodies,
> At distance heard, peopled the milder air.

Al Purdy liked such poetry, but he was no Wordsworth.
His sleeve was rolled up to his biceps and he had no ear for
linnets or any other literary birds. He listened to the voices in
and under his own trees:

> The starlings strut jaunty and raucous
> with just that little swagger which says to hell with
>   you bud

And now how the local people respond to Al's gruff songs!
There are teenagers at the A-frame tearing apart the old
imperfect sun deck and hammering it together again, paint-
ing it and putting the heavy red wooden deck chairs back
on. Meanwhile, at Trenton High School they are studying
Al's poetry, the poems about being bored at school and the
poems about living poor beside a lake, and they are digging
poetry. Al said that he dropped out of school because he was
not improving at football and the only room he liked was the
library. Now the one at Trenton High is called the Al Purdy
Library, and there are already kids in it writing poems. The
art students are planning sculptures and installations for the
library. Not to be outdone, the tech students spent the winter
of 2010–11 on their own Purdy project.

I have mentioned most of the buildings that have been put

up on the Purdy Compound. It is time to mention the most famous outhouse in Canadian literature and photography. Perhaps shoveling is a simpler skill than sawing or hammering, but in the late fifties on a plot beside a sylvan lake in the County, it was equally necessary. The Purdy privy was a one-seater with a pointy roof that, like the workshop and the little pump house, echoed the shape of the A-frame. Al Purdy was an artist as well as a carpenter, after all.

Eventually a chemical toilet appeared indoors, and eventually that was replaced by regular big-city plumbing. But Al liked the outhouse. He went on using it after its successors arrived. It is not unusual for the beginnings of poems to come to poets while they are on the throne. I often wonder whether Yeats's line came into Al's head while he was in the biffy: "I will arise and go now . . ." (Sorry.)

Like a lot of Canadian poets and their families, I used the outhouse back in the day, and I followed the rule ordained by its builder. You were supposed to employ a marker to write your name and perhaps some rural sentiments on the interior wall. It is for this reason that Ottawa poet Seymour Mayne once gave his opinion that Purdy's outhouse should be given a place of honour at Library and Archives Canada. Wordsworth and Yeats, after all, must have had outhouses, but did they immortalize them in verse and photograph?

But back to the tech students of Trenton High School. The English students were reading Purdy poems for credit. The art students were going to decorate the halls. So the tech students wanted in on the act. Why not the outhouse, someone asked as a jest. We can refurbish the outhouse and get credit and have a story to tell our grandchildren, came back the serious answer. The truly enlightened shop teachers opened their eyes wide, and before you knew it, a trailer and crew showed up in the back yard of the cottage. Cameras clicked away as five guys with enviable skill strapped and buttressed the delicate old structure and lowered it gently onto the trailer. Eurithe got them to sign the guest book.

One of the first things the tech students will try to do, I hoped, is to remove the blue paint from the interior walls, because under that paint is Margaret Laurence's autograph, Earle Birney's autograph, Michael Ondaatje's autograph, Irving Layton's autograph. You see why those kids will be earning their credit. What if there is an otherwise unpublished Margaret Atwood poem under that paint? Excitement built at Trenton High, as we anticipated Roblin Lake's version of the Dead Sea Scrolls.

As the venerable edifice on its tidy trailer climbed the grass driveway, I found myself hoping that those students would not do a perfect job. It is not just the cottage that is "never finished." Al did not believe in a Robert Frost-like ending for his poems, no slamming shut, no final word. Some of them seem as if he had just left the typewriter for a while. We are more likely to get an off-hand remark, a contradiction, a question, than any formal closure. Even after the poems were published, Al would be revising them. Readers who notice a similarity between these poems and the lovely dark-skinned A-frame behind the ash trees on a corner of Roblin Lake are feeling that sense. "I say the stanza ends but it never does," wrote Purdy in an early poem.

With the outhouse gone, I returned to spend the rest of the day at my favourite post, in a comfortable chair in the annex, looking out through the giant picture window. The window was intended for a big commercial building in Belleville, but wound up here in the cottage, turned to become horizontal. All the rest of the afternoon, a hornet whizzed his wings and bounced against my side of the glass.

I saw a fat beagle come around to pee on the corner of the front deck. A black squirrel I had been watching for three days took his usual route, up into the trees in the yard, leaping from tree to tree, then back down once he was next door. All the squirrels around that end of the lake know that Eurithe takes no prisoners.

Then I looked up and saw that one of the tall cedar trees down near the water had wide deciduous leaves projecting from its top. What can those be, I asked Eurithe. Wild grapes, she said. I know just the winemaker, I said.

# Purdy Among the Tombs

*Al Purdy and I exchanged letters, as they say, for forty* years,* so of course we had some differences of opinion. The last time I saw him was a week before he died on Good Friday, 2000. It happened that I owed him a letter, so a couple years later I left one for him on his book-shaped headstone at the bottom end of Purdy Lane in Prince Edward County, Ontario.

I never thought that he'd write back. I should have known.

* I think that if I have any place in the history of Canadian poetry, it is as a kind of bridge figure. I have always wanted to make you sure that I belong to a peculiar west coast poetry group or movement that is way out there, but also to be considered part of the newer establishment in Toronto, where Canadian literature is gathered and sent to market. All my adult life I have explained or defended one side to the other.

Something like that geography pertains to time as well. I'm in the old guard and the *avant-garde*. When I came to Canadian poetry, I looked for a tradition that I could squeeze into. But I could not find any Modernism. I was looking for some *sophistication*, and I could not find any. I wanted a poetry that showed the results of intellectual curiosity *and* an understanding that a poem's challenge is to find a form equal to the task.

I did not find this combination in A.J.M. Smith (though I heard him classified as a Modernist!) or Irving Layton or E.J. Pratt. The whole of Canadian poetry, it seemed to me, enjoyable as it might be at times,

So here I am with another letter I owe him. I am really looking forward to his reply this time.


Dear Al:

I was recently leafing through Ontario professor Sam
Solecki's 1999 book about you, a book published by University of Toronto Press, and the first monograph on the poet
in question since my much smaller one published in 1970.
Dr. Solecki's bibliography has a section devoted, as it says, to
"Reviews, Critical Essays, and Books on Al Purdy." Mine is
the only book listed. None of my reviews or critical essays is
listed.

Anyway, the reason for leafing through this book was that
I was hoping to be struck by some observations that might be
useful to my proposed paper about your religion and politics.
Instead, I was reminded of the old self-satisfied, too-early-
satisfied light academic put-down of the Vancouver poets that
has been going on for several decades in the comfortable Eng-

---

was being produced by authors rather than poets. Reading Smith and
Scott and Birney and Page, I kept sensing authority. Their forms were
satisfied and they seemed to have opinions, two qualities one finds in
later years among the presentations of the "slam poets."

The sophistication I was looking for I had found in the USAmer-
ican poets Ezra Pound, Robert Duncan and Robin Blaser. Eventually
I would find some in the work of Margaret Avison and Phyllis Webb.
Poets younger than I have it, unquestionably — people such as Lisa
Robertson and Erin Mouré.

So here I am. I am thought of as far out and without substance by
the neo-con poet-reviewers of present-day English Montréal, and a
tad square by my experimental friends.

When Al Purdy published *Poems for all the Annettes* in 1962, I
jumped on the book and said that it was good news from the east. I
reviewed it and talked it up. I got Purdy an invitation to read at UBC.
Here, I said, was an Ontario poet who wished his lines to enact a
world rather than describing it. I had found someone who wanted to

lish departments of Eastern Canada, or what they call there, Central Canada. I was reminded of a reading I once gave at a university in the Eastern Townships. I had read a long poem filled with passages from writings by others — William Butler Yeats, James Joyce, Jack Spicer, Emily Dickinson, and so on. One of the Eastern Townships professors put on a stern face and asked me why I had not quoted from any poets in my own tradition.

How presumptuous! This person was telling me that a poet from way out west should consider himself a product of a cultural world devised by the Anglo-Saxon halls of learning in Ontario and Quebec, and maybe New Brunswick. This was a person who seemed not to have figured out what the poem was saying. She certainly did not note a difference between quotation and dictation and the implied position of the writer.

A decade or so before that, a group of us was putting out a poetry newsletter called *Tish* (about which some people are still complaining these forty years later) and presuming to offer our musings in poetics as well as our poems. One mes-

---

get a step past the ego-bound Layton and the meter-counting Smith.

It was interesting to read Purdy's next five books. More and more he would become an author, and he would be gathered in by the establishment composed of Toronto publishers, reviewers and professors. The promising sense of the provisional and vulnerable heard in *Annettes* would fade, as Purdy's poems became three-page recordings of Al's travels and the way he felt about them. These were very interesting, and his sly portrayal of the scholar with rolled-up sleeves would turn him into a brand. Followers followed, usually poets who aspired to Purdy's attitude but did not have his erudition. I bought all his books and enjoyed the first-person stories a lot. But I was disappointed — Al loved writing about explorers such as Franklin and Purdy, but as a poet he was not exploring.

No matter. I went to dozens of his readings, wrote him tonnes of letters, joined the legion of poets who could imitate his reading voice. But he was so darned sure of himself. He liked archaeological sites, but his poems were not like them. They were anecdotal and com-

sage we kept getting from back east was that a Canadian poet does not do poetics — a Canadian poet is supposed to be instinctive and a regular guy. The only poet back east who was doing anything much like poetics was Louis Dudek, and sure enough — the publishing and academic businesses went overboard promoting his gonadal associate Irving Layton, leaving Dudek to be called a minor poet.

Dudek's model had been Ezra Pound, author of many books about poetry and culture, including *ABC of Reading*. In our version of Vancouver we liked the fact that poets such as Robert Duncan and Charles Olson wrote poetics that were completely involved with their poetry. In his book about you, Dr. Solecki writes about "the question of who should speak for Canada," a notion that would never had entered our minds out west, where we do not tend to think of poets speaking for a country. Perhaps this is because we do not equate our area with the country. But apparently the notion has currency in Ontario universities. Then Dr Solecki says that you would have opined that William Carlos Williams, like Olson,

---

plete, amusing and touching. They were often dear. But they were never abandoned. And they did not have any holes you could wriggle through.

So no, Al Purdy did not do for me what I'd wanted from him. I surely liked him. I re-read his books a lot, and wrote about them more than you might expect. But Al Purdy was not what they used to call a post-modernist. He wasn't even a Modernist, really. He was in another line that had its spiritual home in the nineteenth century, one that included the writers he so often cited as his reading tradition — G.K. Chesterton, Bliss Carman, Rudyard Kipling, and which he would see continue through anti-sophisticates such as Peter Trower and Charles Bukowski.

And good for him, I say. I really enjoyed the letters Al and I sent one another, badly typed or scrawled combinations of scorn, admonition and comradeship.

"influenced only the minor Canadian poets: Daphne Marlatt not Margaret Atwood, Frank Davey not Michael Ondaatje" (1999, 94). In other words, the Vancouver poets, not the Toronto ones.

That is a view that is easy to maintain if you stay in Toronto, where Sheila Watson, Ethel Wilson and Robert Kroetsch are referred to as western regionalist writers, and where once a year Ontario novelists get dressed up and share a local award called the Giller Prize. Once a decade or so, they'll toss it to a writer in a neighbouring province as long as the writing seems familiar.

Al, you know that there has been a lot of peculiar umbrage taken against the so-called Tish movement over the years, from the lunatic diatribes of Robin Mathews to the insular politics of various maple leaf factions. A common accusation is that the young Vancouver poets collaborated with an entity the academics call "Black Mountain" and its efforts to colonize Canadian poetry. In all the years since these attacks began in the sixties, I have never seen any of the "critics" go to the trouble of reading Charles Olson and offering quotations or even *précises* that would suggest imperial intentions.

Even you, Al, who found ways to praise my poems in print, had to lift me away from my pack, and took part in the unresearched attack on "Black Mountain." (Once a tenured professor in a Canadian English department asked me in all seriousness where in BC Black Mountain is. I replied that it was just back of the North Shore mountains you can see from Vancouver on a sunny day.)

I am like a lot of Canadian poets: I loved you, and often found myself saying "Oh, Al!" I spent all those years writing letters in which I told you why I was a follower of Williams and Olson. And you did once write about our lifetime argument: "Even the disagreements I have with him do not seem dead ends for me, but reasons to re-examine my own reasons for writing as I do" (*SA* 376). I felt the same way, Al. Late in life you did soften a bit on Williams, but in your letters to other people you often retold and edited your erroneous memory of telling Fred Wah that you thought that all Olson had was a good voice. You never, to my knowledge, quoted Olson, to show me where he was at fault. I'm not sure that you have read him.

Olson and Duncan and Louis Zukofsky are hard to read. It's a lot easier to read Frost and Neruda and oh, say, Charles Bukowski. To read one of Charles Olson's lectures you will probably have to have been reading Alfred North Whitehead, Carl Sauer, Pausanius, and the Canadian geophysicist J. Tuzo Wilson. I have not run across a lot of Canadian poets who show any interest in J. Tuzo Wilson.

Olson liked Wilson because he was devoted, meticulous, and accurate, and because he shifted an entire world of knowledge. Here is one of the ways in which Olson talked about that in his 1955 pamphlet *A Bibliography on America for Ed Dorn*: "And to hook on here is a lifetime of assiduity. Best thing to do is *to dig one thing or place or man* until you yourself know more abt that than is possible to any other man. It doesn't matter whether it's Barbed Wire or Pemmican or Paterson or Iowa. But exhaust it. Saturate it. Beat it" (1997, 306-307].

You'll notice that though Olson is literally writing to a poet here, the advice is nowhere near restricted to such a person. But it does serve to exclude a poetry made of passing observations or personal expression.

And I think that you will have to agree that in this pamphlet at least Olson is not looking to recruit any Canadian poets or researchers into his orbit. He wants to hear from people who know more than he does about subjects of interest to them.

From 1964 to 1974, you kept up a correspondence with the USAmerican poet Charles Bukowski, largely about getting drunk or published. In 1983 a book was made of these letters, and in your foreword you said that Bukowski and Robinson Jeffers are the only USAmerican poets you have "much use for" (*BPL* 13).

Bukowski, most people know, is pretty easy to figure out. Skateboard boys try to shoplift his books. While Olson in his letter to Dorn develops a theory drawn from Whitehead's *Process and Reality*, Bukowski, in a 1965 letter to you, has this to say about publishing mimeographed poetry magazines: "We are going to run the g.d. universities and their well-backed dull magazines right out of business and when they come running to our alter [sic] we are going to give them the big dick pissing right into their eye" (*BPL* 29). So if a university conference is anything like a university magazine, and I happen to go to one, I had better tell the academics there to keep their eyes, as they say, open.

In saying that Bukowski is one of the two USAmerican poets worth listening to, you are presumably talking about your own taste, maybe your own poetic, maybe portraying it as anti-intellectual, expressive, manly in a bar-room kind of way. If someone said, "But Al, you have a lifetime's collection of academic-looking books downstairs in your air-conditioned and steel-barred personal library," you would make a cryptic and ambiguous remark, playing the rube playing the scholar playing the con man.

Thirty-five years ago, when I billed you as the world's most Canadian poet, I had that series of masks in mind. Both as a poet and as a Canadian you were playing a game created by groups in the less powerful parts of society. Native people in the interior of BC interact with a sense of humour that white people don't even notice. In the USA the African American people invented language and music that the ofays could only try to make money from.

So you, pal. Given the right time, you might let the university poet know that you have been reading Greek history, but most of the time you will pretend that scholarship is not fitting for a red-blooded Ontario poet.

So when some Canadian poets start reading and codicilling the philosophical thought of a USAmerican poet such as Charles Olson, they have to be betraying what Upper Canadian professors call the Canadian tradition? What propaganda did Charles Olson lay out? We know that he advised learning as much as can be learned about a subject of your choosing. But he was himself omnivorous in his curiosity. For example, in 1953 he mentioned some synthesizing ideas that made use of Alexander Bogomolet's researches into the nature of connective body tissue to prove that human beings were designed to live 130 years.

Certainly a lot of what Olson had to offer was esoteric, but in all his essays and poems the biggest lesson he taught us neophytes was that we should never alienate our attention from our own world, and we should pay close attention to our specific poem-producing bodies. We Tish poets gave up trying to understand how such advice was perilous to our authenticity and sovereignty. Don't colonizers usually try to get the locals to forget their *locus* and accept the colonizers' notion of a tradition? In a NET film Olson cited Heraklitus's complaint that "men are estranged from that with which they are most familiar."

If the poet of some location, say the Tantramar marshes or London, Ontario, will keep his eyes open to his situation, write with the language that is his in that place, and listen for the music that is at the heart of all things, as Thomas Carlyle said, we will want to know his poems. Bring us Gloucester, Massachusetts. Bring us Ameliasburgh, Ontario. Bring it in your language. We will try to send you Vancouver as we hear it.

Now I think I am talking about politics and religion, but what about *your* politics and *your* religion? They are there, in your poetics. I believe that. And didn't you learn some of that from D.H. Lawrence? In *No One Else Is Lawrence!*, a book of commentaries you and Doug Beardsley made in the nineties, you were discussing the poem "There are No gods." You said, "And I believe in the gods of imagination. I believe in them, in the way Lawrence created himself, freed himself from all the fetters that are placed on us, on the human mind. We all know that we live two lives. That we live our public lives in which we talk to each other, live in a way so that we don't get arrested. We also live our private lives, released from all the fetters, in which we think quite different thoughts."

When Beardsley said, "And live different lives. And poetry does this," you replied, "And we get away with as much as we can, if we think it does not offend our morals, our personal morality" (*NEL* 24).

Like you, Charles Olson saw D.H. Lawrence as a completely necessary poet for our time, however long that has been. In a little 1950 essay called "D.H. Lawrence and the High Temptation of the Mind," Olson aimed, as you did, away from the socialized intellectual toward the moral: "Lawrence somehow chose the advantage of moral perceptions to those of the intellect." Olson then developed a complicated analogy or metaphor connected with the race between tortoise and hare, bringing in references to Plato, Ortega, Schopenhauer and others, before saying that "Lawrence knew, as no metaphysician ever does, the discipline and health of form, organic form as distinguished from that false form which the arrangements of the intellect, in its false speed, offer" (1997, 137).

Like you, Olson was possessed of the archaeologist's eye, and you both understood early that the contemporary poet digs as an archaeologist rather than adds as a historian. In your poem "In Etruscan Tombs," you imagine Lawrence and Purdy "clambering over the mossy stones." Olson, in another essay on Lawrence, maintained that Lawrence's visit to the Etruscan Places was the culmination of his lifetime wanderings in search of ideal place, and that he spent the last fifty months of his life imagining it. You probably had something not much different in mind when you finished your poem:

> we scramble out of the tombs
> to follow the well-marked trail
> leading back the way we came from
> the way we came from (*NEL* 102).

In any case, I don't think that Lawrence was engaged in "speaking for England," nor that you, scrambling in Tuscany, were "speaking for Canada."

I plan to go to Tuscany this summer, Al. If I find myself among your "tumbled heaps of earth and stone," I will keep my grave-robber's eye out for both of you.

You know me, Al,

GB

*Books cited*

Beardsley, Doug and Al Purdy. *No One Else Is Lawrence!* Madeira Park: Harbour, 1998.

Bukowski, Charles and Al Purdy. *The Bukowski/Purdy Letters 1964-1974.* Sutton West and Santa Barbara: The Paget Press, 1983.

Olson, Charles. *Collected Prose.* Ed. Donald Allen and Benjamin Friedlander. Berkeley: University of California Press, 1997.

Purdy, Al. *Starting from Ameliasburgh.* Madeira Park, Harbour Publishing, 1995.

Solecki, Sam. *The Last Canadian Poet.* Toronto: Toronto, 1999.

*The Useful Dead*

*Recently I read a newspaper story about a young com-*puter nerd in Florida who has been threatened by the USA military because he runs an Internet website that features pictures of dead human beings in places such as Iraq and Afghanistan. The pictures come from the USA soldiers who have killed the locals and then photographed them with their digital cameras and sent them to Florida via their laptop computers. It seems that they receive free pornography in trade. I suspect that some of the photographers were not really the men or women who bagged the civilians. I bet some of them were just lucky enough to be in the right place at the right time with a camera.

But the authentic ones, the actual killers, remind me of those Hemingwayesque photos we used to see, of a USA hunter in some place such as Africa, holding his rifle and kneeling beside the dead lion or okapi he has dispatched.

In Vietnam, one remembers, the USA soldiers used to cut the ears off the locals they killed, to authenticate the daily death count for USA television. Ears are easier to cut off than scalps, apparently.

So I got to thinking. In the past few years we have heard

a lot of stories of dead people in piles, not only in the Islamic countries that the USA invades, but also in the ones they only bomb, such as Serbia, Libya, etc. We know, too, that the US military has prevented the news media from photographing their recent wars, having seen the deleterious effects of a free press on their imperialist objectives in Vietnam. When a soldier recently leaked a photograph of a planeload of US coffins being sent back to the US, there was a big kafuffle. That got me thinking, too.

The coffins were lined up on the floor of the cargo hold of a C-5 Galaxy. There was nothing loaded on top of them, or under them. And there was a lot of space left on the floor of the cargo hold of that C-5. This got me thinking some more.

But first, let me focus on the other end of the subject I hope to cover here. This year another story about human bodies emerged from the University of California. The university officials are considering inserting barcodes in body parts and cadavers that are intended for use in their medical schools. You have seen these codes on cornflakes boxes and paperback books. They make life easier for checkout clerks who have trouble with numbers. But the barcodes in bodies would not be there for the checkout line, if you will pardon the term — they would help the university fight the black market in dead people. California has been the site of several scandals involving lost and stolen corpses in recent years. An official with the UCLA medical school made $700,000 by selling donated dead people to profiteers. The director of the UC Irvine Willed Body Program was fired after being accused of selling hundreds of spines to private enterprises, which in the United States include big hospitals.

The black and grey markets for lifeless human beings are enormous. There may be a lot of people in the world, but only a small percentage gets used after death. Most of these are willed by their former owners, are gifts of their relatives, or unwanted items from state institutions. There are more and more medical schools coming into existence, and demanding cadavers for their anatomy classes.

In England, Henry VIII passed a law saying that only the corpses of executed prisoners would be allowed into the dissection rooms of British colleges. But by the early nineteenth century, there were not enough hangings to supply the hospitals, and in 1832 the British government passed a bill making it legal for hospitals to acquire bodies from poorhouses and relatives of the deceased. The most recent legislation is the Human Tissue Act of 2004, whereby all acquisition of corpses for medical use is regulated by the Human Tissue Authority. Presumably the days of the grave robbers are over.

But the day of the refrigerator robbers is here. A shortage aggravated by the medical professors who are looking for something on the side has led some medical schools such as University of California at San Francisco to cut cadavers out of their curricula. University directors say that medical students just do not have the time to go to all the work of dissecting human remains. Freshmen today have too much on their plates to spend precious hours at the old hands-on work. Besides, UCSF spends $1,700 on every corpse it has to embalm and store. Either the medical schools have to dispense with dissection the way the faculties of arts and humanities have dispensed with Latin and English grammar, or they have to find new sources of cadavers while protecting the ones they already have.

Medicals schools are not the only outfits that want bodies. There are also the manufacturers and testers of bicycle helmets, automobile airbags, passenger jets, and so on. There are a thousand and one uses for a dead human body, especially if it is intact and relatively fresh. Around the time of the savage French Revolution, Dr Joseph Guillotin perfected his compassionate head-chopper with the use of corpses. A little over a century later the French army stood corpses up and used them as targets for tests on their new rifles.

The industrial revolution was to bring with it all sorts of uses for new cadavers. Crash test dummies are familiar gadgets in the automotive safety business, but if you want to make detailed tests of car crash trauma to human tissue and bones, you have to get a dead man or woman or child into the SUV. You have likely seen pictures of retired passenger jets used in mock crashes and runway fires; you probably did not know that the airplane may have had a lot of expired human bodies strapped into their seats. They have been into space with NASA, too.

If you would like to know more juicy stories about the expired, get a copy of Mary Roach's book *Stiff*. It is full of amusing stories about the author's visits to historical records and present-day cold rooms. A particularly colourful example is her visit to a plastic-surgery instruction lab, where she encounters forty severed heads lying face up in roasting pans. Each student is assigned two of these heads, presumably to give him or her another stab at a botched procedure. In all likelihood the headless corpses are being stored in the walk-in refrigerator, where they await their usefulness in the liposuction class. Timing is important when it comes to the human body's natural inclination to biodegrade. It is a nip-and-tuck business.

Even in its biodegradability, though, the human corpse can be used in contemporary experiments. In a lovely hickory wood next to the medical school at the University of Tennessee, human beings engaged in their long sleep lie on their backs. They are research tools in an academic study of human decay. The lovely wood is also home to songbirds and insects.

Of course, once the people get well into decay, there is no question that they have become lifeless but part of the greater life of nature. Other kinds of bodies offer less in the way of clarity. Most readers are aware of the old controversy about the definition of death. Students with the goal of becoming surgeons are fortunate that most doctors' organizations lean towards the notion of death as the absence of brain activity. Other things, such as hearts and lungs, can be kept going by the application of industrial inventions, so that those lucky students can benefit from the lessons to be learned from "heartbeat cadavers."

You will remember that these students are overly busy, and sympathize with them when they fall asleep over their assigned reading about biomedical ethics. But you should also know that in the first years of anatomy labs, people held solemn funeral services for the bodies they were going to dissect. Sometimes the relatives of the deceased took part, leaving before the professor began his instructions.

Well, these relatives were probably comforted more than those who more recently donated their dead "to science," not knowing that they might easily be sold to the military to be used in the testing of land mines.

Which leads me back to what I was writing about at the beginning of this discussion. Remember those soldiers in Asia Minor who are sending back Internet photos of the humans they have bagged? Remember how much more room there is in the cargo holds of the big planes used for flying the US dead back to America?

Why not scoop up the carcasses of the men, women and children who have been so unfortunate as to stand in the way of democratization, and ship them to the Universities of California and London and other institutions with body shortages? There might be some social conflict at the harvesting end, but in a war a lot of the niceties do not make the cut. Perhaps the cadavers can be claimed as spoils of war. Perhaps the US Corps of Engineers could work out an exchange system — a mile of paved road for each specimen, for example.

Negotiations with the rifleman or tank commander might be more complex. Surely a soldier who receives free pornography for a few photographs of his prize will expect a good deal more for the trophy itself. This brings up the whole question of free enterprise versus big government. In the USA the government that usually heaves away a lot of public money claims to be in favour of tax reduction and spending cuts. A program would have to be worked out, so that privatizing will appear to work at both ends, for the harvester and the user.

Of course government would have to play its part. Private companies do not own enough C-5 Galaxies, and it is only by electing and influencing cooperative governments that corporations can get wars started across the world. But the biomedical companies, though not as big as some of the petroleum companies, for example, should quickly be able to learn the system.

Still, the medical schools grow apace, and other users of body parts proliferate. Sometimes military invasions may not be able to keep up with demand. This is where the masters of international trade will need to step in and do their part. At any given time, and dependent on the season, there will be natural disasters taking place somewhere on our globe. With our cautious approach to instituting fuel emission controls, there will be more. Massive floods, earthquakes, tornadoes, soccer riots and the like provide fluctuating sources of bio-medical materials. These events generally take place in exotic locales, in countries that could use some Western money. Chances are that rescue organizations such as the International Red Cross or the United Nations will need to hurry people to these disaster sites. A major problem for developers is always the presence of human bodies; they delay efforts to provide drinkable water and survey new roads, and so on. If a company that wins a competition for a federal contract can get in there and clear out the no-longer-living, the collateral damage can be limited

Of course the unfortunate country will need to be compensated. There might also be unforeseen problems, as is so often true when one is dealing with non-Western heads of state. A tinpot dictator in a backward country in South America or Asia might act slowly in response to a natural disaster, hoping to maximize the returns. The business of government, we have been told so often and so wisely, is business.

The gathering of human clutter is an idea whose time has come. During the Second World War both German and Japanese doctors made shameful experiments on living human beings who happened to be members of defeated groups. Meanwhile millions of corpses were being dumped into mass graves or family crypts. Such hideous scenarios can and should be avoided.

In recent times there has been a lot of talk about stem cell research and human cloning — some medicos imagine refrigerator rooms filled with manufactured cadavers, the advantage being that these objects will have lungs and blood systems that are working, an obvious benefit in the Anatomy 101 laboratory.

The harvesting of the inutile dead, it seems to me, goes a long way toward solving at least two of the major problems confronted in our contemporary world.